# BENINGBROUGH HALL

*North Yorkshire*

Jacob Simon

THE NATIONAL TRUST

This new guidebook is very largely the work of Jacob Simon, Curator of Eighteenth-century Paintings at the National Portrait Gallery. He has written Chapters 1–5 and the picture entries in Chapter 7. Anthony du Boulay has written Chapter 6, and Tony Lord, a former Gardens Adviser to the National Trust, Chapter 8. Roger Whitworth, Historic Buildings Representative for Yorkshire, has thoroughly revised Chapter 7, which is based on the previous guidebook by the Trust's Architectural Adviser, Gervase Jackson-Stops. The National Trust is also very grateful to members of the Dawnay family for their assistance, and to the following, who have helped in various ways: Ray Barker, Terry Friedman, Ivan Hall, David Howarth, Dr Oliver Impey, Peter Scott, Mary Thallon and Elizabeth Treip.

© 1992 The National Trust
First published in Great Britain in 1992 by National Trust Enterprises Ltd, 36 Queen Anne's Gate, London SW1H 9AS
Registered charity no. 205846

ISBN 0 7078 0136 2

Photographs: *Country Life* pages 20, 26, 47, 50, 71; Courtauld Institute page 15 (bottom); Coverdale and Fletcher Ltd page 31; James Dawnay/Broadsword Publishing page 24; House of Lords Record Office page 9; National Portrait Gallery, London pages 34, 35, 36, 37, 38, 39, 40, 41, 42, 43, 58, 61, 72, 73, 77, 79, 81, 82; National Trust pages 22, 23, 87; National Trust Photographic Library/Niall Clutton pages 13, 15 (top), 32; NTPL/Andreas von Einsiedel pages 6 (bottom), 16, 29, 33, 45, 49, 56, 57, 60, 62, 63, 67, 68, 69, 70, 75, 84; NTPL/Angelo Hornak page 12; NTPL/Horst Kolo pages 11, 46, 53, 55, back cover; NTPL/Ian Shaw pages 1, 86, 89, 90, 93; NTPL/Derrick E. Witty front cover, pages 6 (top), 8, 17, 18, 19, 21, 25; Sotheby's page 4.

Designed by James Shurmer

Phototypeset in Monotype Lasercomp Bembo Series 270 by Southern Positives and Negatives (SPAN), Lingfield, Surrey (8356)

Printed in Italy by Amilcare Pizzi s.p.a.

# CONTENTS

se firent a besances deuant le duc
de lancastre. puis parle dune cõ
clusion que prindret le duc de lan
castre et le roy de portugal pour
aler en castille. Chap. xii.

E duc de lancastre se
iournant en la cite
de besances messire
regnault de roye enuoya par
vng herault demander a messi
iehan de hollande vng fait dar

# CHAPTER ONE

# THE EARLY BOURCHIERS

The manor of Beningbrough lies in the flat water meadows of the River Ouse some 7 miles to the north-west of York. Like so many estates in England, Beningbrough has a history stretching back beyond the Norman Conquest. Before the Normans the manor had belonged to Asford, who is the earliest known owner of Beningbrough, but by 1086 it was in the hands of Hugh, son of Baldric.[1] In the Domesday Book it was called Benniburg, a name which is thought to be Old English, meaning Benna's fortified place.[2]

In the twelfth and thirteenth centuries, much of what is now the Beningbrough estate passed to a religious establishment, the Hospital of St Leonard at York, which, with 206 beds, was one of the largest of its kind in Britain.[3] To provide funds for its work, the hospital's master and thirteen chaplain-brothers held numerous estates in Yorkshire and the North. At Beningbrough a valuation of the manor made in 1287, apparently the only detailed survey of the estate between Domesday and the Dissolution of the Monasteries, shows that the hospital owned some 540 acres, which were farmed to provide food for its needs.[4]

In 1539 the last Master of St Leonard's, Thomas Magnus, felt obliged to surrender the hospital and all its lands in the face of pressure from Henry VIII, but in return he received a pension which allowed him to retain Beningbrough for life. He died in 1550, as rector of Sessay church, 10 miles north of Beningbrough, and is commemorated there by a brass. The estate then came to John Banester who had purchased it from the crown in 1544 subject to

*'A Tournament held before the Duke of Lancaster'; from an early sixteenth-century edition of Froissart's 'Chronicles'. Sir Ralph Bourchier's grandfather, Lord Berners, produced the first English translation of Froissart's famous history of the Hundred Years War*

Magnus's life-interest.[5] Thus the change in possession at Beningbrough was part of the greatest revolution in land ownership in England since the Norman Conquest. It was Banester's nephew, Ralph Bourchier, who inherited the estate at his death in 1556, so starting the long Bourchier connection with Beningbrough.

Ralph Bourchier's father, James, was the illegitimate son of John Bourchier, 2nd Lord Berners, Chancellor of the Exchequer in 1516 and one of the Knights who attended Henry VIII at the Field of the Cloth of Gold in 1520. However, Berners's most lasting achievement is his masterly translation of Froissart's *Chronicles*, published in 1523, the first into English of this famous history of the Hundred Years War. The Bourchiers had been one of the most illustrious and powerful of English noble families in the fourteenth and fifteenth centuries. Lord Berners numbered among his ancestors Robert de Bourchier, who was made Lord Chancellor in 1340 by Edward III and fought at Crécy under the Black Prince, and Thomas Bourchier of Knole, Archbishop of Canterbury, who officiated at the coronations of Edward IV, Richard III and Henry VII.[6]

In later life Lord Berners fell upon hard times financially and felt obliged to leave England in 1520 to become Lord Deputy of Calais, a position he held until his death in 1533. At Calais his son, James Bourchier, lieutenant of the outlying castle of Ambleteuse, married Mary Banester, another member of the local English community. Their son Ralph was chosen by John Banester, Mary's brother, as heir to his estate at Beningbrough.

Ralph Bourchier built all or part of Elizabethan Beningbrough on a site near the present house.[7] He was 25 when he inherited the estate in 1556, at which time the property was let to Sir Leonard

*Sir Ralph Bourchier, painted in 1582. He built the Elizabethan manor house which once stood near the present house (private collection)*

In later life Ralph Bourchier rose to a place of some prominence in Yorkshire: he was High Sheriff in 1580–1, knighted in 1584, and an MP for the county in 1589. At his death, most of his property went not to his elder son, William, who was declared insane, but to one of his grandsons. The eldest of these, Robert, died unmarried at the age of eighteen in 1606, so it was to William's second son, John, that Beningbrough passed. Since he was then under age, the estate was put in the jurisdiction of the Court of Wards, an action which was later to have unfortunate consequences.

*Marquetry panel from the Elizabethan house bearing the initials of Sir Ralph Bourchier and his first wife, Elizabeth Hall. It is now set into the panelling of the Great Staircase*

Beckwith of Selby, Receiver of the Court of Augmentations in Yorkshire.[8] Bourchier had previously inherited estates in Staffordshire from his father and in 1571 was first elected to Parliament as MP for Newcastle-under-Lyme. It is not known exactly when he moved to Beningbrough, but between 1568 and 1575 he sold most of his land in Staffordshire and was certainly at Beningbrough by 1576. Bourchier's Elizabethan house apparently lay some 300 yards south-east of the present hall.[9] In the absence of any plans or records of its appearance, one can only surmise that it was a red-brick manor house on a modest scale, a house of the gentry rather than the nobility, with perhaps half a dozen main rooms, many of them panelled. The most tangible evidence of his occupation is the Elizabethan panelling which was later reused to finish some of the second-floor rooms in the present house. One of the panels can be dated before 1577, the year when Ralph Bourchier remarried, for it is inlaid with the initials 'RBE', which link his name with that of his first wife, Elizabeth Hall.

# BOURCHIER FAMILY TREE

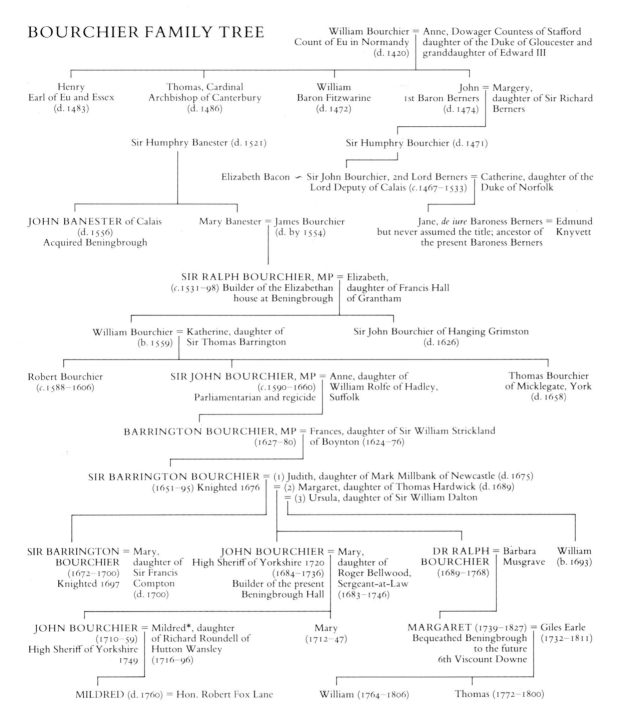

William Bourchier = Anne, Dowager Countess of Stafford
Count of Eu in Normandy | daughter of the Duke of Gloucester and
(d. 1420) | granddaughter of Edward III

Henry
Earl of Eu and Essex
(d. 1483)

Thomas, Cardinal
Archbishop of Canterbury
(d. 1486)

William
Baron Fitzwarine
(d. 1472)

John = Margery,
1st Baron Berners | daughter of Sir Richard
(d. 1474) | Berners

Sir Humphry Banester (d. 1521)

Sir Humphry Bourchier (d. 1471)

Elizabeth Bacon ⌐ Sir John Bourchier, 2nd Lord Berners = Catherine, daughter of the
Lord Deputy of Calais (c.1467–1533) | Duke of Norfolk

JOHN BANESTER of Calais
(d. 1556)
Acquired Beningbrough

Mary Banester = James Bourchier
(d. by 1554)

Jane, de iure Baroness Berners = Edmund
but never assumed the title; ancestor of    Knyvett
the present Baroness Berners

SIR RALPH BOURCHIER, MP = Elizabeth,
(c.1531–98) Builder of the Elizabethan | daughter of Francis Hall
house at Beningbrough | of Grantham

William Bourchier = Katherine, daughter of
(b. 1559) | Sir Thomas Barrington

Sir John Bourchier of Hanging Grimston
(d. 1626)

Robert Bourchier
(c.1588–1606)

SIR JOHN BOURCHIER, MP = Anne, daughter of
(c.1590–1660) | William Rolfe of Hadley,
Parliamentarian and regicide | Suffolk

Thomas Bourchier
of Micklegate, York
(d. 1658)

BARRINGTON BOURCHIER, MP = Frances, daughter of Sir William Strickland
(1627–80) | of Boynton (1624–76)

SIR BARRINGTON BOURCHIER = (1) Judith, daughter of Mark Millbank of Newcastle (d. 1675)
(1651–95) Knighted 1676 | = (2) Margaret, daughter of Thomas Hardwick (d. 1689)
= (3) Ursula, daughter of Sir William Dalton

SIR BARRINGTON = Mary,
BOURCHIER | daughter of
(1672–1700) | Sir Francis
Knighted 1697 | Compton
| (d. 1700)

JOHN BOURCHIER = Mary,
High Sheriff of Yorkshire 1720 | daughter of
(1684–1736) | Roger Bellwood,
Builder of the present | Sergeant-at-Law
Beningbrough Hall | (1683–1746)

DR RALPH = Barbara
BOURCHIER | Musgrave
(1689–1768) |

William
(b. 1693)

JOHN BOURCHIER = Mildred*, daughter
(1710–59) | of Richard Roundell of
High Sheriff of Yorkshire | Hutton Wansley
1749 | (1716–96)

Mary
(1712–47)

MARGARET (1739–1827) = Giles Earle
Bequeathed Beningbrough | (1732–1811)
to the future
6th Viscount Downe

MILDRED (d. 1760) = Hon. Robert Fox Lane

William (1764–1806)

Thomas (1772–1800)

Owners of Beningbrough appear in CAPITALS

* Her sister, Catherine, married Christopher Dawnay, brother of John Dawnay, the grandfather of the 6th Viscount Downe, who inherited Beningbrough in 1827.

*Sir John Bourchier, who owned Beningbrough in the first half of the seventeenth century (private collection)*

This John Bourchier was born in about 1590 and knighted in 1619. Of the Beningbrough Bourchiers he is the only one to stand out above the run of worthy Yorkshire squires, for he played a prominent part in national events.[10]

Sir John was an eccentric and highly irascible individual, determined to fight for his rights and beliefs whatever the consequences. A puritan, he was described by a contemporary as 'a serious person, an open professor of religion'. His early career was overshadowed by battles with the Court of Wards over his estate. He was the most prominent of the few North Riding landowners who refused to pay the forced loan which Charles I levied in 1627 so as to avoid having to seek funds from Parliament.

Sir John's greatest foe was no less a person than Thomas Wentworth, the future Earl of Strafford and a fellow Yorkshireman. As President of the Council of the North from 1628, Strafford per-suaded the King to agree to give up the centuries old Royal Forest of Galtres and to create a thousand-acre deer park. Sir John claimed that this enclosure infringed on common rights long held by the Bourchiers and their predecessors in title. Though he accepted 95 acres of moorland in compensation for 'all his pretence of title', Sir John found a way of carrying his complaint in person before the King by deliberately pulling down the fences while Charles I was hunting in the park in the summer of 1633. Strafford wrote of the case, saying 'as concerning Sir John Bourchier and his insolent carriage, it is his daily bread, the man is little better than mad, one grain more would weigh him down to a direct Fury'. For his offence Sir John was heavily fined and imprisoned until October 1634. He never forgot this indignity. Seven years later, after Strafford's fall from power, Sir John was revenged when his case formed one of the lesser charges against Strafford, who was convicted and executed for treason.

In the Civil War, Sir John wholeheartedly supported the Parliamentary cause, organising the local militia and acting on the committee of the Northern Association for the defence of Yorkshire and adjoining counties. Through his mother, Katharine Barrington, he was related to Sir Thomas Barrington, the Parliamentary general, and to Oliver Cromwell himself. High Sheriff of Yorkshire in 1645 and MP for Ripon in the Long Parliament from 1647, Sir John was chosen to be a judge at the trial of Charles I in 1648. On 27 January 1649 he was one of 49 judges who passed sentence of death on the King.

At the Restoration he faced trial and execution like other regicides, but died in December 1660 while his case was still pending, asserting to the last the justice of the King's condemnation: 'I tell you it was a just act; God and all good men will own it.'

Sir John's son, Barrington Bourchier, was named after his grandmother's family, the Barringtons of Essex, staunch Puritans. There were to be three successive Barrington Bourchiers at Beningbrough between 1660 and 1700.

The first Barrington rescued the family estates from the threat of forfeiture. Like his father, he held a number of local offices during the Common-

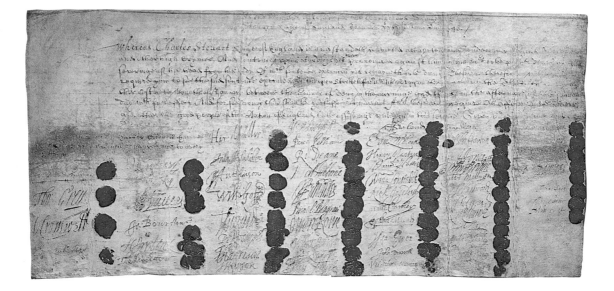

*The Death Warrant of Charles I, signed by Sir John Bourchier*

wealth, but he lacked his father's strongly puritan spirit and decided to take up the cause of Charles II. He was persuaded by his wife's uncle, Sir Henry Cholmley, to join in Sir George Booth's abortive insurrection against the Commonwealth in August 1659 'on assurance that his father's offence would be no prejudice to him if he would so assist'. In the disorder which followed Oliver Cromwell's death, General Monck marched south from Scotland to reinstate the Long Parliament and secure new elections. On his southward march he was met and welcomed to York by Barrington Bourchier, recently High Sheriff of the County, who was prominent among those who signed the Yorkshire declaration in support of a free Parliament in February 1660. As a result of his boldness, Barrington was deprived of office and apparently imprisoned, albeit only briefly. For when new elections were called in April 1660, he was chosen to sit as the MP for Thirsk. It was this Parliament, the first to be elected since 1640, which invited Charles II to return from exile.

At the following election Barrington did not stand, retiring from public life, safe in the knowledge that his estates were secure. These he con-siderably expanded during the 1660s, purchasing the adjacent manors of Overton and Shipton. At the same time he must have set about enlarging Bening-brough, for an increase from six to eleven hearths was recorded in the Hearth Tax Returns between 1662 and 1665. What was the source of his wealth? His income, as far as it is known, places him in the ranks of the upper gentry. The family's fortunes were firmly based in the land. Once Beningbrough was out of the jurisdiction of the Court of Wards, sound estate management, for which the Puritans were renowned, must have revived the property. To this may be added the profits of office held during the Commonwealth and compensation for damages, if ever actually received, from Strafford's estate. In the next generation the family's fortunes were to be further enhanced by a number of favourable marriages.

Barrington's son, the second Barrington, was knighted by Charles II at Newmarket in 1676 at the age of 25. Like his father, he devoted his energies to local affairs and his own estates. In the tumultuous year of the Revolution in 1688, he was not alone in losing his position – he was deputy lieutenant of the North Riding – only to have it restored later the same year, when James II realised that his aims were not to be achieved by bullying. Sir Barrington died aged 44 in 1695. He was survived by his third wife and by five sons aged between two and 23. Three of those sons, Barrington, John and Ralph, were to come into the estate over the course of the next 65 years.

An intriguing glimpse of Beningbrough before the house was rebuilt by John Bourchier comes from the inventory of Sir Barrington's personal estate at his death.[11] Of the eighteen rooms in the house, the two most richly furnished were the Best Lodging with a blue damask bed, the contents being valued at the considerable figure of £45 5s, and the tapestry-hung Green Room with a bed upholstered in green and eight matching chairs. Much of the inventory is devoted to the kitchen quarters, stables and home farm. No less that £667 10s of the estate's total value of £1,413 was in ready money, kept in various bags and purses 'in the drawers: in Sr. Barrington's Chamber'.

In April 1697, less than two years after his father's death, Barrington Bourchier, the third of this name, was knighted by William III at Kensington Palace. Little is known of his short tenure at Beningbrough but that he had ideas for improving the appearance of the estate. This is evident from his correspondence with the 'ingenious' Thomas Kirke of Leeds, whom Sir Barrington compliments on the 'delicate cutts and ridings' in his wood at Moseley, asking him 'to doe something of that nature' for Beningbrough.[12]

This Sir Barrington married well. His wife, Mary Compton, was the daughter of Sir Francis Compton, Lieutenant-Colonel in the Horse Guards and a son of the 2nd Earl of Northampton. But tragedy followed: Barrington's first son was buried in 1699; Barrington's brother, Mark, died in December the same year, only to be swiftly followed by his wife and second son and by Sir Barrington himself some months later.

Thus at the age of only sixteen, John Bourchier, Barrington's half-brother, came into the estate. He was the eldest surviving son of Sir Barrington senior and Margaret Hardwick. His mother had died in 1689, when he was but five, and his father in 1695. Though he was named as heir and sole executor in the will of his half-brother, Sir Barrington junior, he was too young to act and he 'spontaneously and voluntarily' chose his aunt, Elizabeth Clavering 'for

tutor and guardian'. All four of his brothers and half-brothers went to Trinity College, Cambridge, but no record survives of John's education. However, we do know that at the age of 20 he set off to Italy on a Grand Tour which was to fill him full of ideas for a new house at Beningbrough.

### NOTES

1 William Page (ed.), *Victoria County History of the County of York*, ii, 1912, pp. 276, 313.

2 A. H. Smith, *The Place-Names of the North Riding of Yorkshire*, English Place-Names Society, v, 1928, p. 19.

3 Francis Drake, *Eboracum*, 1736, p. 334; William Page (ed.), *Victoria County History of the North Riding*, ii, 1923, p. 162; Royal Commission on Historical Monuments, *An Inventory of the Historical Monuments in the City of York, The Central Area*, v, 1981, pp. 93–5.

4 'Beningbrough in 1287', typescript on National Trust files, drawn from Acc. 162 QQ1, York City Archives (original in Staffs R.O.).

5 L. P. Henry VIII, xiv, part 2, p. 227; xv, p. 455; xix, part 1, p. 77. For Magnus see British Library, Lansdowne MS 980, f. 71 and Add. MS 32490, Y41.

6 R. E. C. Waters, *Genealogical Memoirs of the Counts of Eu in Normandy 996–1350 and of the English Earls of Eu of the House of Bourchier 1419–1540*, 1886. For Lord Berners, see also Arthur Collins, *Baronies by Writ*, 1734.

7 For an excellent account of the owners of Beningbrough from the late sixteenth to the early eighteenth centuries, see Pat Taylor, 'The Restoration Bourchiers of Beningbrough Grange', *Yorkshire Archaeological Journal*, lx, 1988, pp. 127–47.

8 For Beckwith, see Taylor, op. cit., p. 127, n. 1.

9 The site is marked on the first edition 6 in Ordnance Survey map of 1852. A limited trial excavation in 1984 revealed orange-red bricks of a type current in the mid- to late sixteenth century. See R. P. Cross, *Archaeological Field Report: Beningbrough Hall*, 1984 (typescript on National Trust files).

10 For Sir John Bourchier, see J. T. Cliffe, *The Yorkshire Gentry from the Reformation to the Civil War*, 1969, pp. 293, 302–3, 346–7, 350.

11 See Taylor, op. cit., pp. 142–6 for the full inventory.

12 For Mr Kirke's wood, see Joseph Sprittles, 'Links with Bygone Leeds', *The Publications of the Thoresby Society*, lii, 1969, pp. 80–2; Barrington's letter, dated 17 January 1697, is in the British Library, Stowe MS 747, f. 87.

# CHAPTER TWO

# THE BUILDING OF BENINGBROUGH

Beningbrough is an enigma. It is one of the most remarkable Baroque houses in England, standing proud in the flat landscape, the façades a bright red brick ornamented with stone, the interiors richly carved and finished. But almost nothing is known of its building history. In 1927 Guy Dawnay, the last owner to hold the house by descent, declared that 'no papers about the building of Beningbrough have ever been discoverable'.[1]

What we do know of Beningbrough is that it was built for John Bourchier after his return from Italy and marriage to a wealthy Yorkshire heiress, that William Thornton, a talented carpenter-architect from York, was responsible at least for supervising the construction, and that the house was substantially complete by 1716. Unless family papers or designs are discovered, it may be difficult to say much more with true conviction.

It was once thought that the house was by Sir John Vanbrugh. If clearly not attributable to Vanbrugh himself, Beningbrough undoubtedly shows his influence in its planning. More recently it has

*John Bourchier, the builder of Beningbrough. This overdoor portrait attributed to Jonathan Richardson (54) is in the Drawing Room*

been suggested that Thomas Archer, one of the few British architects with first-hand knowledge of contemporary Baroque buildings in Rome, may have given advice on the more Italianate features of Beningbrough's design. But as we now know that John Bourchier visited Italy, it seems quite likely that he himself played a major part in the design. The early eighteenth century was a time when an interest in architecture was an acceptable accomplishment for a young man.[2] Whatever the precise process at Beningbrough, the strong influence of recent Italian architecture on the form and decoration of the exterior of the house makes it clear that Bourchier's two-year tour of the Continent was of central importance in forming his taste.

It was probably in the summer of 1704 that the 20-year-old John Bourchier set out for Italy on the Grand Tour, an experience which by then was coming to be seen as an essential part of the education of a rich young man. By 1 September he had reached Padua where his name is to be found inscribed in the book of visitors to Padua University as 'John Bourchier of Yorkshire'. By 25 September Bourchier was in Rome, recorded as 'lately arrived from England' by the 1st Duke of Shrewsbury.[3] The Duke, long resident in Rome, kept a constant watch for English visitors, as his journals reveal. On 9 November he notes: 'All the English gentlemen in

town dined with me. We were 14 at table.' This presumably included Bourchier, who called on the Duke again in December and on 21 April the following year, 1705. If Bourchier needed a mentor in this city of riches, he could not have found a more knowledgeable fellow-countryman than the Duke, who had gone out of his way to study the Baroque churches and palaces of Rome. The Duke is known to have been in touch with the prolific publishing family, De Rossi, and may therefore have been responsible for showing Bourchier Domenico de Rossi's newly published *Studio d'Architettura Civile*, a volume which appears to have been an important influence on the appearance of Beningbrough. Bourchier was still in Rome towards the end of the year, and seems to have been well provided for, if we can judge from a letter sent home by another young Yorkshireman, Viscount Irwin of Temple Newsam. Writing from Rome on 5 December 1705, Lord Irwin complains of the meagreness of his funds, regretting how he is 'much inferior in everything than Mr Boucher, who has tho' but a gentleman, a greater allowance than I'.

Bourchier probably returned home in 1706. Two years later at the age of 24 he married Mary Bellwood at Acomb parish church in York. It was 'the long expected match' of 'a dapper couple', according to Anne Clavering, Bourchier's child-

*'A Punch Party', 1760; by Thomas Patch (Dunham Massey, Cheshire). Patch's caricature shows a group of English gentlemen on the Grand Tour enjoying the pleasures of Italy. John Bourchier must have been entertained in much the same way by the Duke of Shrewsbury in Rome*

*The south front*

hood friend (she was his guardian's stepdaughter).[4] A year older than her husband, Mary had like him been left an orphan, at the age of eleven on the death of her father, Roger Bellwood, Sergeant-at-law in York and London. It was perhaps the marriage settlement which provided John Bourchier with the security to embark on the expensive task of building a new house. Kiveton, a Yorkshire house comparable in size to Beningbrough, had been completed a few years earlier at a cost of over £15,000.

At Beningbrough the site chosen was a very slight rise above the general level of the Ouse flood plain, not far from the Elizabethan manor. This would probably have remained the home of John and Mary Bourchier and their two young children while the new house was being built. The speed of construction would have depended on the scale of Bourchier's resources, but, judging from the pace of work on contemporary houses, building and fitting out may well have taken five or six years. This would imply that Beningbrough was begun in 1710 or 1711. By May 1714 – the earliest documented mention of the new house – the building was well enough advanced for the glazing of the windows to be all or part complete. The house was presumably substantially finished and fitting out well advanced by 1716, the date on the elaborate marquetry roundel on the half-landing of the Great Staircase.

In the Saloon there was once a pair of overdoors by Jacob Bogdani dated 1720, suggesting that the furnishing of the house may have taken a number of years to complete.

William Thornton, the supervising architect at Beningbrough, was born in about 1670 and trained as a carpenter and joiner. His name is linked to the Bourchiers and so to Beningbrough by two eighteenth-century sources, a list of Yorkshire houses within a copy of *The Builder's Dictionary* of 1734 in the Metropolitan Museum, New York, where he is described as architect of 'Mr Bourchier's', and letters from him to the agent of a later Earl of Strafford. Writing on 5 May 1714 about his work at Wentworth Castle, he recommends glazing bars of 'ye same thickness I have done for Mr Bourchier & others'. In August the same year he mentions having 'wainscotted most of ye rooms at... Mr Bourchiers'.[5] The monument erected in St Olave's church in York at Thornton's death in 1721 refers to him specifically as 'Joyner and Architect'. The fact that the arms of the Joiners Company also appear on his tomb suggests that he may have been trained, or worked for a time, in London. As joiner he is known to have worked on the fitting out of several Yorkshire houses during the first two decades of the eighteenth century, not only Wentworth Castle, but also Bramham Park (for the 1st Lord Bingley), Castle Howard (for the 3rd Earl of Carlisle) and Sir Charles Hotham's house at

# PLANS OF THE HOUSE

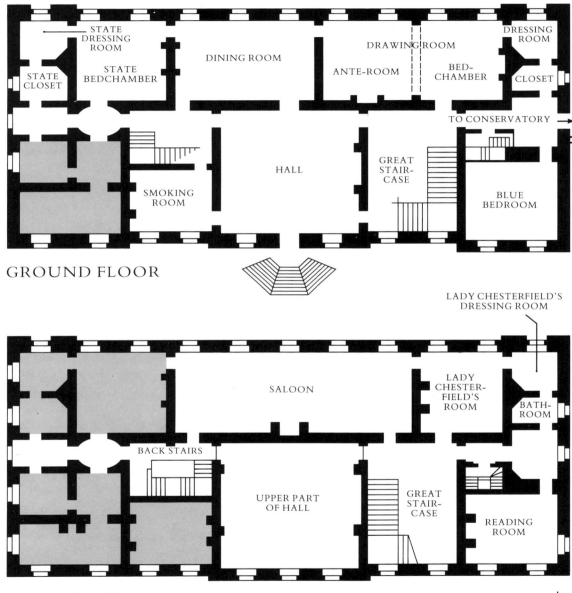

GROUND FLOOR

FIRST FLOOR

Shaded areas not open to the public

Beverley. He also had some practice as an architect, like a number of talented craftsmen of the York school ('Workmen advanc'd to the degree of Architects' as Hawksmoor patronisingly put it). He restored the north transept of Beverley Minster in 1716–20 but, apart from his work at Beningbrough, his only other recorded commissions as an architect are for minor buildings at Swinton Park and Ledston Hall, both in Yorkshire.

In the formality of its planning, Beningbrough bears resemblance to a number of other grand Baroque houses of the period. The house is laid out on strong cross-axes, with central doorways on the north and south fronts opposing each other and transverse corridors running the length of the house from east to west on the two principal floors (see plans of the house, p. 14). Beningbrough has a monumental entrance hall on the north front rising through two storeys and a line of state rooms along the garden front which faces south. This is the pattern promoted by Vanbrugh and which Thornton would have seen at Castle Howard where he worked between 1708 and 1711.

Externally, the compact rectangle of the house is plain and lacks a grand portico or pediment. The use of red brick with architectural details in stone is firmly in the English tradition and would have been less expensive than building entirely in stone as at Castle Howard or Bramham. The chief material used for Beningbrough is a hard crusted brick, made locally from the different coloured alluvial clay beds along the banks of the Ouse. The finely pointed principal fronts are a combination of red and orange, while the screen walls and pavilions flanking the forecourt are in another kind of brick, paler, less carefully graded in size, and laid with rough mortar – suggesting that they were built a few years either before or after the main block. The bricks are of exceptionally small size, about 9 by 2 inches.

In a rather old-fashioned way the main façades consist of two equal storeys raised on a low basement. But for all its apparent simplicity the

*(Left) The central window on the north front is based on an engraving of Bernini's Palazzo Chigi in Rome from the first volume of Domenico de Rossi's 'Studio d'Architettura Civile', published in 1702*

15

exterior has several unconventional features which are very obviously derived from Italian sources, and in particular the engravings of Roman palaces to be found in a number of recently published volumes. It is here that John Bourchier's contribution to the design is likely to have been most pronounced. The use of massive console brackets to support an overhanging cornice, even down to the idea of inset windows, is found at the Palazzo Altieri, illustrated in Ferrerio and Falda's *Palazzi di Roma*.

Another idea which can be traced to Ferrerio and Falda's volume is the choice of alternatively raised and recessed strips of dressed stone – an unusual form of quoining – to mark the slight projections in Beningbrough's façades; on the garden front these quoins are restricted to the end bays as on Borromini's College of the Sapienza at Rome. The curious window frame above the entrance door, with curved ears and a central fluted triglyph as a keystone, comes from Bernini's Palazzo Chigi in Rome, reproduced in the first volume of Domenico de Rossi's *Studio d'Architettura Civile*, published in 1702. Similar window frames are found at Heythrop in Oxfordshire, the house begun in 1707 by Thomas Archer for the Duke of Shrewsbury, whom Bourchier had of course met in Rome. The pairs of massive scaled wooden console brackets supporting the frieze at Beningbrough, terminating in dentils of the Doric order, are also paralleled at Heythrop House (and at St Paul's, Deptford, designed by Archer in 1712), although they may be based on one of 'Trois diferents Corniches' en-graved by Daniel Marot in his *Nouveau Livre d'Ornements* (of about 1700) rather than on an Italian source. In the absence of any Bourchier family papers, it is difficult to determine the circumstances exactly, but it is possible that Archer, as an amateur gentleman-architect, may have given advice to John Bourchier on various points of detail (as he did with Lord Strafford at Wentworth) and that Thornton acted as executant architect-cum-builder.

Once the house had been roofed and the windows glazed, attention would have turned to the fitting out of the interior. Again there was some attempt to save expense, for the Hall is painted plaster above a plinth of stone rather than stone throughout, as in some grander Yorkshire houses. It is in the profusion of superb woodwork and carving in the state rooms leading off the Hall that the interiors are at their richest. The carving is as remarkable in its way as Samuel Watson's at Chatsworth or John Seldon's at Petworth, approaching at times the assurance of Grinling Gibbons himself. Thoresby, writing in 1702, refers to work which 'the most celebrated Gibbons wrought at York' with the mason-architect John Etty, and the skill shown by the York school of carvers here may therefore derive from first-hand contact with the greatest craftsman of the day.

Although no accounts survive for Beningbrough, we know the names of a few highly skilled craftsmen who worked with Thornton elsewhere. At Wentworth Castle his chief assistant (and later his successor) was a French Huguenot craftsman, the

*Detail of the intricate woodcarving in the Drawing Room cornice*

*Bouttats and Chapman's 1751 painting of Beningbrough shows large service blocks flanking the main house, which have now gone (private collection)*

wood-carver Jonathan Godier (anglicised to Good-year). It is easy to point to small similarities in the two houses – for example, the paired cornice brackets in the Drawing Room are found at Wentworth, as are the lambrequins or draped plinths which ornament the overdoors. Thornton also regularly worked with another Huguenot, the stone- and wood-carver Daniel Hervé (or Harvey), who may perhaps have carved the great stone coat of arms over the garden door to the house. During the early eighteenth century there was a flourishing school of Huguenot craftsmen at work in the North, many of them exiled from France as Protestants following the Revocation of the Edict of Nantes in 1685. Given Thornton's close association with such craftsmen, it is not surprising to find that the dominant influence at work in the panelled rooms at Beningbrough is French. Many features of

the wood carving have their origins in recent French publications, and in particular the engraved work of Jean Berain and his pupil, the Huguenot Daniel Marot, who left France for Holland and became architect to William III. However, it was probably only the carvers at Beningbrough who were French. The magnificent wrought-iron grilles in the Hall have been attributed stylistically to the famous Derbyshire blacksmith Robert Bakewell. Another craftsman linked with Thornton, and so probably with Beningbrough, is the York plasterer John Bagnall who worked at Castle Howard and at Hotham's house at Beverley, and who was to be one of Thornton's executors in 1721.

Rather plainer in style than the house are the two small flanking pavilions built of brown brick. These buildings cannot be much later in date than the house itself, for they are to be seen in Samuel Buck's drawing of Beningbrough made between 1719 and 1723 (reproduced on p. 87). More problematic are the large pedimented service blocks shown facing each other across the forecourt in the only early painted view of Beningbrough, dated 1751. Were they ever built? It has been suggested that this painting is no more than a record of a scheme for proposed additions. But if so, why are the two blocks shown with mullion-and-transom windows which were quite out of fashion by the mid-eighteenth century? It seems more likely that John Bourchier had these rather unadventurous service quarters built at the same time or very soon after the main house, and that they were pulled down when the existing stable block was built in the late eighteenth century.

Of John Bourchier's later life remarkably little is known. He was High Sheriff of Yorkshire in 1720 as his grandfather had been before him and his son was to be after. He took an interest in the York races, subscribing to the stake money, and he also sub-scribed £25 in 1730 to a venture of particular importance in York's eighteenth-century history, the building of the Assembly Rooms. John Bour-

*John Bourchier the younger; by John Vanderbank, 1732 (private collection). Bourchier lived at Beningbrough in the mid-eighteenth century and also built Micklegate House in York, where he was a leading figure in local society*

chier died in 1736 at the age of 52, leaving one of the grandest new houses in Yorkshire as his monument.

He was followed at Beningbrough by his son, also John, who in 1738 married Mildred Roundell in York Minster. She was the co-heiress of a rich landowner, Richard Roundell of Hutton Wansley. This John Bourchier and his wife feature promi-nently in York society. He was High Sheriff in 1749 and he built one of the finest town houses in York, Micklegate House, completed in 1752. At that time the city was the main focus for cultural life in the north of England, and various county families preferred to make York rather than London their home when not staying on their estates. In the summer the Bourchiers would sometimes be found staying in Bristol or taking the waters at Bath. And it was at Bath that John Bourchier died in 1759, aged 49. Sadly his only child, Mildred, died the following year within months of her marriage to Robert Fox Lane, the son of the MP for York.

Micklegate House became the home of John Bourchier's widow, while Beningbrough was claimed by his uncle, Dr Ralph Bourchier, then aged 71, a successful physician who had made London his home. He agreed to pass his interest in the house and the 7,000 acre estate to his only daughter, Margaret Bourchier, who was to live at Beningbrough for the next seven decades.

NOTES

1 *Country Life*, lxii, 1927, p. 772.

2 Derek Linstrum, *West Yorkshire Architects and Architec-ture*, 1978, pp. 28–9, 61–6.

3 Horatio F. Brown, *Inglesi e Scozzesi all'Università di Padova dall'anno 1618 sino al 1765*, Venice, 1921, p. 186; Historical Manuscripts Commission, *Report on the Manu-scripts of the Duke of Buccleuch & Queensberry*, ii, part 2, 1903, pp. 784–8 (for the Duke's journal); Johnny Madge, 'A "Virtuoso" in Rome: Charles, Duke of Shrewsbury', *Country Life*, clxxiii, 1983, pp. 232–3; Leeds District Archives, Temple Newsam papers, unlisted (4th Viscount Ingram, bundle 9).

4 H. T. Dickinson (ed.), 'The Correspondence of Sir James Clavering', *Surtees Society*, clxxviii, 1967, p. 13.

5 British Library Add. MS 22238 f. 150, dated 5 May 1714 (not March 1714) and f. 166.

# CHAPTER THREE

# THE LATER OWNERS OF BENINGBROUGH

Over the next two centuries Beningbrough did not change greatly in outward appearance, but the Bourchiers were to be succeeded by three other families: the Earles by the marriage of Margaret Bourchier to Giles Earle in 1761; the Dawnays by inheritance from Mrs Earle in 1827; and Lord and Lady Chesterfield by purchase in 1917. If there is any pattern to these years, it is rather as before: worthy people with strong local interests who rise occasionally to some slightly greater prominence on a broader stage.

Of all the owners of Beningbrough, it was Margaret Bourchier, the last of her line, who held the house for longest, over 65 years in all. She married Giles Earle at Hendon in Middlesex in 1761, when the *York Courant* described her as 'an Heiress with a very great fortune'.

The Earles were an unconventional couple. One acquaintance called her 'this curious woman...such a complete Gig that I was quite entertained with her'.[1] Her husband was the son of a Whig MP, but, unlike his father or grandfather before him, he took little part in public life. A French visitor to Beningbrough in 1768 acknowledged him as 'a good judge of character, with an exquisite sense, of free and strong opinions', but noted his pessimistic view of his fellow beings and his boastfulness about himself.[2]

Probably the year after this visit Beningbrough was shut up and the family left for the Continent. What led the Earles, by then both in their thirties and with one child, to venture abroad for several years is not known. It seems that they made a lengthy stay in Paris before going on to Italy. The Earles were in Rome by November 1770 where they met Dr Charles Burney, the historian of music, and they spent much of the summer of 1771 at Cardinal Albani's villa at Castel Gandolfo, close to

the Pope's summer palace.[3] In December that year the antiquary James Byres wrote to Sir William Hamilton, British envoy at Naples, reporting their departure, adding his opinion of the Earles: 'They are, I really think, good natured well meaning people, and had they not lived at Paris some time would have done very well.'[4] Their Italian souvenirs included a bust of the Pope, Clement XIV, by Christopher Hewetson, which still sits on the Hall chimney-piece at Beningbrough, a set of views of Naples and Vesuvius by Pietro Antoniani, dated 1771, and a marble vase supplied by Piranesi, who dedicated to them three plates in his series of

*Giles Earle in middle age; from a late eighteenth-century miniature (private collection). He married the last of the Bourchiers, Margaret, in 1761, soon after she inherited Beningbrough*

etchings, *Vasi, Candelabri, Cippi...*, first published as a collection in 1778.[5]

That Margaret Earle came back home with continental airs emerges from an amusing letter written by Theresa Parker of Saltram to her brother, Frederick Robinson of Newby Park, in 1774.[6] Mrs Earle is described as being 'dressed very French' and speaking in 'as broken English as if she had never seen England for more than two months'. Her manner 'is so far improved that as before you could only be amused with her absurdities, she is kind enough to carry them to the highest degree'. At Beningbrough the Earles appear to have experienced a financial crisis. The estate was mortgaged for £12,000 in 1777, and in the following year one correspondent wrote of Giles Earle's precipitate departure for Calais, having paid off all his servants. A rather unlikely, but colourful account in a later novel, *Beningbrough Hall*, published in 1836, implies that Beningbrough was used in some kind of way for secret dealings with France. It was probably only after the sale of Hendon House in 1785 that the Earles' financial situation eased, and what few improvements they made at Beningbrough, such as the stables and the new lodge at Newton, probably belong to the period of their greater prosperity.

'If you wish to see Mrs E. in all her glory, you must look in at the ball this night', wrote Giles Earle in 1805 to his solicitor, Joseph Munby at York, who was evidently something of a friend as well as a man of business. These few surviving letters written between 1802 and 1806 provide a rare glimpse of Giles Earle's character in old age. He deemed money well laid out if 'the result shall be neatness or convenience in the roads or grounds contiguous to or leading to Beningbrough Hall'. But he complained of his tenants' requests for farm improvements: 'I dare indeed hardly venture out my house, being way-laid ... by numerous petitioners for petty favours who covet my posts & rails and timber, and would equally covet my ox & my ass, if I had any.' As time went on, it was his own wellbeing which was his abiding concern: 'My health hangs, like a Mahomet's coffin, between heaven and earth, with a preponderancy rather to earth but I hope to escape both being *on* the turf and *under* it *this year*.'

Giles Earle did not die until 1811 at the age of 78. His two sons had predeceased him, fighting in the war against Napoleon. Who was to inherit Beningbrough? Mrs Earle's choice fell on the Rev. William Henry Dawnay, the future 6th Viscount Downe, and when his first son was born in 1812 she acted as

*The stable block was put up by the Earles, probably after 1785*

godparent.[7] Not only were the Dawnays distantly related to the Bourchiers by marriage (through Margaret Earle's cousin, the last John Bourchier), but William Henry Dawnay had been a close friend of her elder son at Eton.[8]

Margaret Earle died at Beningbrough in October 1827 at the age of 87. To use the words of the epitaph added to her husband's monument in Hendon Church, 'Mrs Earle was the last of one of the most ancient families in England; the Bourchiers having their origin from the remotest period of antiquity.'

From 1827 to 1916 Beningbrough was owned by the Dawnays, an old Yorkshire family with a strong tradition of service in Parliament, the Church and the Army. The principal Dawnay residence was Cowick Hall in the West Riding and later Wykeham Abbey near Scarborough. Remarkably few alterations were made to Beningbrough in the

*Lydia Dawnay; by F. R. Say, 1854 (private collection). She inherited Beningbrough from her father, the 6th Viscount Downe, in 1846, and lived there with her brother, Payan, for the next 44 years*

*Newton church was rebuilt by Lord Downe in 1839 and rebuilt again by Lydia and Payan Dawnay ten years later. A late nineteenth-century postcard of the church*

Victorian period, perhaps because the house was used as a secondary residence, usually occupied by a younger son of the family.

William Henry Dawnay, the heir to the Beningbrough estate, was the second son of John Dawnay, 4th Viscount Downe, a Whig MP for 20 years. Like many a younger son Dawnay went into the Church, becoming Rector of two family livings in Yorkshire in 1796. At the age of 55 he inherited Beningbrough and five years later in 1832 he became 6th Viscount at the death of his elder brother.

Lord Downe resigned his church livings and moved to Beningbrough with his wife, Lydia. They made various improvements to the house and grounds in the 1830s.[9] It was probably at this time that a gallery was installed over the Hall to improve circulation at first-floor level, and two ground-floor rooms amalgamated to form a decent-sized drawing-room of the sort which had by then become necessary for entertaining. One other change was not of Lord Downe's making: the opening of the York to Newcastle railway in 1841, with a station close to Beningbrough, heralding the decline of the River Ouse as a commercial waterway.

Lord Downe died at Beningbrough in 1846, worth £80,000, and his widow followed him two years later. Cowick went to their first son, the 7th Viscount, while the Beningbrough estate was in-herited by the younger son, Payan Dawnay, and his sister, another Lydia, who together shared Beningbrough for more than forty years. Little happened to the house in their time, for brother and sister lived quietly, devoting themselves to public-spirited activities and the welfare of their tenants.

The Dawnays of this generation were great church builders. The 6th Viscount rebuilt Newton Church in 1839. His eldest son, the 7th Viscount, made a vow to build three new churches when he married Mary Bagot, the daughter of the Bishop of Bath and Wells, in 1843. He was an early patron of the High Victorian architect William Butterfield, commissioning from him a series of churches in Yorkshire and Rutland, and some remarkable estate housing. At Lord Downe's premature death in 1857, Butterfield described him as 'a most really good man and a great loss in many ways though he lived in so retiring a manner'.[10] His brother and sister at Beningbrough, Payan and Lydia, followed his example, rebuilding three local churches – Shipton, Newton (again) and Overton – between 1848 and 1855, to the designs of the Yorkshire railway architect G. T. Andrews. They also built and maintained two local schools, and modernised cottages and tenant farms on the estate.

Lydia Dawnay died aged 76 in January 1890 and her brother, Payan, aged 75 in June the following year. The estate was inherited by their nephew,

Lieutenant-Colonel Lewis Payn Dawnay, the second of the six surviving sons of the 7th Viscount. With his coming, Beningbrough was transformed. For the first time in more than a century the house and gardens reverberated to the sound of a young family: skating on the pond in winter and cricket weeks in summer, amateur theatricals in the Hall, battledore and shuttlecock in the gallery, 'tobogganing' down the main staircase, house parties and entertainments.[11]

In 1877 Lewis Dawnay had married Victoria Grey, granddaughter of Lord Grey, the prime minister and champion of the great Reform Bill of 1832. Soon afterwards he resigned his commission in the Coldstream Guards and in 1880 was elected to Parliament for the Thirsk Division, which he continued to represent until 1892. At the time of inheriting Beningbrough, he and his wife and four young children were living at Bookham Grove, near Dorking, a property which had long been in the Dawnay family. For a time Beningbrough was let, but in August 1892 the Dawnays moved in, making it their main home. Over the next two decades rather more than £18,000 was spent on improving the house and its surroundings. Electricity was installed for the first time, and every farm on the estate (about 45 in all) was modernised at a total cost of £13,500.[12] The Conservatory and a new service wing, subsequently demolished, were added in 1892 at a cost of £7,725 under the direction of the architect Colonel R. W. Edis, known for his work in the Queen Anne style. The forecourt was remodelled the following year, when the iron gates were hung by Starkie Gardner at a cost of £119.

The house became a centre of political as well as social activity, for Colonel Dawnay continued to campaign actively for the Conservatives after he had ceased to be a local MP. However, his attempts to form a Yorkshire Corps of Gentleman Volunteers to assist the Irish Loyalists in the face of Gladstone's second Home Rule Bill in 1893 fell on unreceptive ground. The Colonel was a man of firm convictions and strong temper. 'He was a very impatient and restless man, known in the family as "The Fidgets"', according to his grandson, Christopher Dawnay.[13] At his death in 1910, the *Yorkshire Evening Press* obituary called him 'somewhat brusque and abrupt in manner... He was extremely outspoken and not overgiven to mincing words; so his political and other opponents might reckon on getting it straight from the shoulder.'

Colonel Dawnay left two sons and two daugh-

*Colonel Lewis Dawnay with his wife, Victoria, and their four young children, photographed about the time he inherited Beningbrough*

ters. The elder son, Major-General Guy Payan Dawnay, had fought in South Africa during the Boer War and in 1906 he married Cecil Buxton, daughter of Francis Buxton, at one time Liberal MP for Andover. When Guy Dawnay inherited Beningbrough in 1910 at the age of 32, he made good his earlier intention and left the army to take up a career in merchant banking. In his diaries he emerges as a more thoughtful man than his father, an innovator and reformer during his army days, a Liberal with a commitment to the 'public services' and a business-man professing no feeling for money for its own sake. He was also an early supporter of the National Trust through his friendship with Nigel Bond, its then Secretary, and pledged his support for the Trust's first country house appeal in 1906, when Barrington Court in Somerset was at risk.[14]

At the outbreak of war in 1914 Guy Dawnay was recalled to the army, eventually joining the British Expeditionary Force to Palestine which led to the capture of Jerusalem in 1917. Dawnay was Deputy Chief of Staff to General Allenby and a brilliant intelligence officer, playing a leading role as strategist for the Palestine campaign. His unusual character is revealed by T. E. Lawrence in *The Seven Pillars of Wisdom*:

Dawnay was mainly intellect... Dawnay's cold, shy mind gazed upon our efforts with bleak eye, always thinking, thinking. Beneath this mathematical surface he hid passionate, many-sided convictions, a reasoned scholarship in higher warfare, and the brilliant bitterness of a judgement disappointed with us, and with life. He was the least professional of soldiers, a banker who read Greek History, a strategist unashamed, and a burning poet with strength over daily things.

In June 1916 Dawnay was in England on leave, probably at Beningbrough where his wife spent much of the summer, and it was then that they decided to sell the house. The sale took place in his absence later that year. For a time there were rumours that the house would be pulled down. Perhaps for this reason Dawnay suggested to his wife in January 1917 that the Government should take it over to let as flats to impoverished war widows or disabled officers: 'There must be so many who would love to live cheaply in beautiful surroundings... and if it were possible one would not feel the *waste* of that beautiful house'.[15]

*Guy Dawnay played a leading part in the Palestine campaign during the First World War. He sold Beningbrough in 1916*

Why did Guy Dawnay sell Beningbrough? Apart from needing the money – the duty on his father's estate was not finally paid off until after the sale – his chosen career as a merchant banker meant that he had to be near London. He did not wish to be an absentee landlord and his wife seems not to have liked Beningbrough. After the war he bought Longparish House in Hampshire and returned to business, becoming chairman of a number of leading companies and starting his own merchant bank, Dawnay Day.

The Beningbrough sale took place at the Festival Concert Rooms, York, in November 1916. The estate of 6,100 acres was broken up by the purchaser, a Cambridgeshire farmer and speculator, William Abel Towler. It had cost him only £137,000, a price which reflected the years of agricultural depression. The Hall, Home Farm and Park, some 375 acres in all, were later sold on privately to Lady Chesterfield for the very low sum of £15,000. With her husband, Lord Chesterfield, she took possession of the house in July 1917. Thus Beningbrough entered an Indian Summer at a time when the country house was coming under increasing threat.

Lady Chesterfield was born Enid Edith Wilson, the fourth of seven children of a wealthy ship owner, Charles Wilson of Hull, and his wife Florence Wellesley, a great-niece of the 1st Duke of Wellington. A Liberal MP for many years, Wilson had built up the Wilson Line into the largest privately owned shipping company in the world; he was created 1st Baron Nunburnholme in 1906, the year before his death.[16]

Wilson's four daughters were wealthy heiresses, and their mother was determined that they should marry well. In 1900 at the age of 21, Enid married Edwyn Francis Scudamore-Stanhope, 10th Earl of Chesterfield, an eligible bachelor rather more than twice her age. He was a Privy Counsellor who had held posts in the Royal Household, and a Liberal like her father. He had probably first met his future bride five years earlier when he acted as best man at the wedding of her elder sister. The Chesterfields lived at Holme Lacy in Herefordshire until 1909 when Lord Chesterfield sold his ancestral home for nearly £200,000 and moved to London. Quite why Holme Lacy was sold and quite why they then chose the war years to move to Beningbrough is not entirely clear. Perhaps Lady Chesterfield wished to be closer to her mother at Warter Priory.

The Chesterfields furnished Beningbrough in great style with pictures, furniture and Gibbons carvings from Holme Lacy, as can be seen in the *Country Life* articles on the house in 1927. By this time much had been done to adapt Beningbrough to their tastes. In the Hall the gallery was removed and the pilasters marbled. The Dining Room was walnut-grained and the architectural details picked out in gold, while in the State Bedchamber and the Drawing Room the panelling was stripped, after the fashion of the day, to reveal the pinewood. A lift was installed in the back staircase and the Saloon painted a strident peacock blue. It is not known who was in charge of the work, but John Cornforth has suggested that it was strongly influenced by Lenygon & Morant, the architectural decorators who pioneered the renewal of interest in early English interiors.[17] Morant & Co. restored the State Apartment bed, when it was still at Holme Lacy, and the labels of the merged firm have been found on the bed in Lady Chesterfield's Room.

*(99) Enid, Countess of Chesterfield; by Ellis Roberts, 1900 (Reading Room). The Chesterfields bought Beningbrough in 1917 and furnished it lavishly with pictures and furniture from Holme Lacy*

Lord Chesterfield was 68 in 1922 when he retired from his court appointment as Master of the Horse to George V. He seems to have spent much of his time in London apart from his wife, and their marriage was childless. When he died in 1933, the title passed to his brother only to become extinct some years later.

Lady Chesterfield's enduring interest was the stud farm which she had set up at Beningbrough in the early 1920s. It was her mother Lady Nunburnholme's interest in racing which led her to change from breeding hunters to thoroughbreds, building up the stud to nine or ten brood mares. The most distinguished foal was Sun Castle, a black colt which Lady Chesterfield had the pleasure of leading in after it won the St Leger in 1941. This was her finest hour.

During the Second World War Beningbrough was requisitioned for use by airmen stationed at the RAF base at Linton-on-Ouse, $2\frac{1}{2}$ miles away. The best of the furniture and pictures were locked up and Lady Chesterfield moved out to the Home

*The Hall in 1927, as furnished and decorated by the Chesterfields*

Farm. Of the bomber squadrons based at Linton, the most famous was 76 Squadron under Wing-Commander Leonard Cheshire VC, who had just completed his book, *Bomber Pilot*, and was already a legendary figure. From time to time Cheshire would visit Beningbrough to see that all was well – and to listen to Lady Chesterfield's complaints about airmen trampling her vegetable garden.

For the men who slept on the top two floors and used the ground floor as a mess, Beningbrough was an oasis of peace. Sergeant Clifford Hill, a gunner in one of the seven-man crews of the great four-engined Halifax bombers based at Linton-on-Ouse, has left his reminiscences of his time at Beningbrough in 1943. Losses were heavy with almost nightly raids over Germany as far afield as Munich. But a safe return brought another world. 'After debriefing and breakfast the seven of us would cycle in the early morning to a dawn chorus along country lanes to Beningbrough.' Later in 1943 Linton became home to two squadrons of the Royal Canadian Air Force, 426 'Thunderbird' Squadron and 408 'Flying Goose' Squadron.

After the war it took some time for the York firm of Walter Brierley to put the house in good repair, but in 1947 Lady Chesterfield, now aged 69, moved back into her old quarters. Many of those who worked on the estate or knew the house have left their own account of her character. Miss Constance Seabrook, the lady's maid who had to dress her three times on hunting days, recalls her demanding standards: 'I never had a hunting lady before, I nearly packed it in, then she seemed a bit kinder and I settled down and mastered her frantic ways.'[18] Those of her former servants who have recorded their memories agree that, though eccentric in her ways, she was a fair and kind employer.

Lady Chesterfield died at Beningbrough in November 1957 at the age of 79. Though she had expressed a wish that Beningbrough should remain in the family, she seems to have understood that this was unlikely to be possible. There were death duties to pay and, as with so many estates in this post-war period, very little in the way of ready assets to meet liabilities. So her executors decided to offer the house to the Treasury. Lady Chesterfield was to be the last private owner of Beningbrough.

## NOTES

1 The fullest account of the Earles is to be found in *Three Yorkshire Villages*, 1973, pp. 15–23.

2 A transcript of H. B. Lemprere's account of his visit to Beningbrough belongs to the Dawnay family.

3 Percy A. Scholes (ed.), *Dr Burney's Musical Tours in Europe*, i, 1959, pp. 236, 297.

4 Chichester–Constable MSS, East Riding R.O., as transcribed by Sir Brinsley Ford.

5 The five paintings by Antoniani are recorded in catalogues of the Dawnay sales, Christie's, 3 December 1892 and 30 May 1919, as are a pair of views of Lake Albano by H.P. Dean and a landscape by Solomon Delane of 1774.

6 British Library Add. MS 48218, f. 200.

7 MS notes inside Bible belonging to the Dawnay family.

8 The two boys were classmates for nine years. See R. A. Austen Leigh (ed.), *Eton College Lists 1678–1790*, 1907. 'How Beningbrough came into the possession of the Dawnays', MS by Lewis Payn Dawnay in the possession of the Dawnay family.

9 None of the improvements is documented. A floorboard recently removed from the Saloon was found to be dated 1833.

10 Paul Thompson, *William Butterfield*, 1971, p. 45.

11 See Guy Dawnay's MS diary for 1894 in the possession of the Dawnay family.

12 See Lewis Payn Dawnay's MS notebooks for 1892–1910 (donated to the National Trust by Alan Pryce-Jones).

13 Alan Bott, *The Dawnay Photograph*, 1986, unpublished typescript, p. 19. The most useful account of the Dawnays at Beningbrough.

14 MS diary for 1906 in the possession of the Dawnay family.

15 Imperial War Museum, Dawnay correspondence, box 69/21/2. See also *'Beloved Beningbrough'. The Dawnays of Beningbrough Hall*, text of lecture given by P. T. Scott and P. Swannell at Beningbrough, 1991.

16 See William Palmer, *Last Lady of Beningbrough*, c.1987, unpublished typescript, for much useful information on the Chesterfields at Beningbrough.

17 John Cornforth, *The Inspiration of the Past: Country House Taste in the Twentieth Century*, 1985, p. 54.

18 Palmer, op. cit.

# CHAPTER FOUR
# THE RESTORATION OF BENINGBROUGH

Beningbrough came to the National Trust in June 1958. The house and estate had been accepted by the government in lieu of death duties at a cost of £29,250, using the National Land Fund (the fore-runner of the National Heritage Memorial Fund). The 1950s were a time when land prices were still depressed, and in retrospect the period has come to be seen as a low point in the fortunes of the country house. It was a decade when numerous great estates were sold, the houses demolished or converted into schools or hospitals, and their contents dispersed. It was also the decade when the National Trust took on more great houses than at any other time in its history – some three or four a year.

When Beningbrough came to the Trust it was almost devoid of contents. In a great four-day sale held some months after Lady Chesterfield's death, those contents not retained by the family were dispersed at auction.[1] Given the limited funds available and the widespread feeling then held that the Chesterfield furnishings, as relatively recent introductions, had no special association with the history of the house, the Trust's objectives at the auction had to be strictly limited. They were, as Robin Fedden, the Trust's Historic Buildings Secretary, recorded after the sale, 'to obtain those essential furnishings which might not make it impossible to let the house to a tenant and which would also provide an essential background to any furniture of our own which we might be able to put in – in other words, carpets, curtains, chandeliers, grates'.[2] In these circumscribed aims the Trust was most successful, managing also to buy the few family portraits in the sale, the great state bed from Holme Lacy and the fine marquetry pier-tables and glasses in the Drawing Room. The Trust's Honorary Representative in Yorkshire, George Howard of Castle Howard, wrote to Robin Fedden: 'the gossip . . . was that the only people who were bidding for these objects were ourselves and the Wills for Ditchley.' The 1950s were a period when fine things could still be obtained at country-house sales cheaply. The total cost of nearly £10,000 came from the National Land Fund.

The Trust's early years at Beningbrough were not easy ones. Derelict outbuildings in the Laundry courtyard had to be demolished. The house, sparsely furnished as it was, presented a rather melancholy spectacle despite a certain grandeur. A curator was installed in 1961 when the house was first opened to the public but this arrangement was terminated in 1967, principally as a result of the difficulties of making opening pay its way on this basis. In 1968 the house was let to a tenant with the obligation to open to the public a number of afternoons a week, but this arrangement, though it brought more income, did not prove a satisfactory way of showing such a grand house. Visitors declined to no more than 2,000 a year and there were problems with the opening arrangements. By the mid-1970s the feeling was widespread that a new approach was needed. 'Dowdy and shabby' and 'a disgrace to the National Trust' are descriptions which were used.[3]

There was a further problem: finance. Beningbrough was the second of six major houses accepted by the National Trust from the government between 1957 and 1977 without any endowment to cover running costs.[4] The understanding was that the annual shortfall would be made good through the agency of the Historic Buildings Council. On acquisition the annual costs were estimated at £2,430 and the income at £630. By 1976 the deficit had risen to £30,000 a year. So when a plan was proposed to improve the appearance of the house, attract more visitors and reduce the deficit, the idea was widely welcomed.

The house was to be put into a good state of repair, the interiors restored and more fully fur-

*The great state bed from Holme Lacy was bought back for Beningbrough when the contents of the house were sold after Lady Chesterfield's death in 1957*

nished, the gardens replanted and a range of visitor facilities added in the outbuildings. The property was close to York with its many visitors and not far from the great urban centres of Leeds and Bradford. The aim was no less than to transform this 'cinderella' of Trust properties into a major tourist attraction. In the event the whole process was to take almost four years from conception to completion.[5]

One of the very first problems to be faced was the dearth of contents. Here the National Portrait Gallery came to the Trust's rescue. In June 1975 the Trust's Historic Buildings Secretary, St John Gore, approached Dr John Hayes, the Gallery's Director, for a substantial loan of portraits. The first joint venture between the two institutions had been at Montacute House in Somerset where an array of fine Tudor and Jacobean portraits had recently been hung in the Long Gallery. At Beningbrough a rather different scheme was devised so that portraits of the late seventeenth and early eighteenth centuries could be shown throughout the house, with a special didactic display on the second floor. Important as the pictures were, the Trust also had to rely extensively on bequests and gifts of furniture. Some of the outstanding walnut furniture at Beningbrough was left to the Trust by the late Lady Megaw in 1974, and a collection of oriental porcelain was given in 1975 by Miss Dorothy Bushell. More recent loans of ceramics, from the Ashmolean and Victoria & Albert Museums, have also enriched the interior of the house.

It was not until January 1976 that detailed planning could begin. By February 1977 all the preliminaries were complete, and Martin Stancliffe was appointed architect. Over the next two years, the roof leadwork was completely renewed, the top floor strengthened and dry rot at first-floor level eradicated. Then new services and security systems were fitted throughout with great care so that they did not impinge on the appearance of the building. Stancliffe was also responsible for the relaying of the Hall floor in stone and the re-ordering of the Dining Room panelling, the stripping out of the Edwardian liftshaft from the back stairs and the development of the second floor to form a portrait gallery.

When it came to the redecoration of the interiors the initial plan was to employ John Fowler, who had worked extensively for the Trust elsewhere. Following his visit to Beningbrough in November 1976, Lady Chesterfield's Dressing Room was redecorated, but sadly Fowler was forced to withdraw from further work shortly before his death in 1977. He was succeeded by David Mlinaric, who had begun working seriously on the decoration of country houses and historic interiors a few years before. Since Beningbrough, Mlinaric has gone on to supervise a whole series of important schemes, including Spencer House in London.[6]

It was widely agreed that work must begin with the Hall, occupying the whole centre of the house and flowing through into the great transverse corridors on both the main floors. In Lady Chesterfield's time the pilasters and the fireplace had been marbled and many other features painted or enriched. However, investigations in 1977 revealed that the plinths to the main pilasters were originally of simple dressed cream-coloured limestone; above that level all decoration had been carried out in plasterwork, probably painted in stone and off-white, in the manner of many other great halls of the period. The plinths and the chimney-piece were stripped of later layers of paint and used to provide the key to the rest of the colour scheme. At the same time the oak floor, a discordant later insertion, was removed for reuse in the restaurant and replaced by stone flags in two colours chosen to match those already in the staircase hall.[7] The overall result was to emphasise the architectural qualities of the space.

What is now seen at Beningbrough is very much an attempt to re-create the spirit of the house rather than a restoration of its precise appearance at the time it was built. Much of the usual evidence for attempting an authentic scheme of redecoration was not available. There were no accounts, no inventories, no plans – a complete lack of documentary evidence. However, research into the original paint colours, begun in August 1977 by Ian Bristow, proved of some help in those rooms which had not been stripped to the bare pine earlier this century. Examination of cross-sections of the layers of paintwork in the Hall, Dining Room, Great Staircase and Saloon revealed extensive use of shades of white, off-white and pale-grey, typical of early eighteenth-century interiors.

There were many difficult decisions still to be made about the appearance of the interior, not made easier by the shortage of funds. The rooms along the south front on the ground floor were the subject of much debate. Could the Drawing Room, made up from two rooms in the 1830s, be put back into its component parts? What should be done with the rooms where the bare pine panelling, originally painted, had been exposed by Lady Chesterfield in the 1920s? Should the doorway from the Dining Room into the State Bedchamber, panelled over last century, be opened up?

To look at this last question first, the decision was taken to reopen the doorway for practical and aesthetic reasons. Not only did this make it possible for visitors to make a circuit through the main rooms, essential in view of the numbers expected, it also restored the magnificent original enfilade view along the length of the rooms on the south front, a matter of great importance for understanding the layout of a Baroque house like Beningbrough.

The next stage in the decision-making process concerned the Drawing Room. Investigations showed that so much had been altered – the panelling, the doorways and even the position of one of the fireplaces – that it would have been difficult to restore the room to its two constituent parts without great expense and considerable new work. The money was not available for this kind of operation. So a virtue was made of necessity: the room records an important social change in the use of the house. Another matter considered to be of great importance to the showing of the ground floor was the visual impact of the south-front rooms as a sequence: the State Bedchamber, the Dining Room now accessible from the bedchamber, and then the Drawing Room. The first and the last of these were in stripped pine and the middle room

*Restoring the Saloon. The Chesterfields had painted the room peacock blue. The National Trust has returned to the original pale grey colour scheme with the capitals picked out in gold leaf*

*The intricately carved cartouche above the garden entrance has recently been restored*

was at that time walnut-grained in a rather unsophisticated way. It was decided that with limited funds only the Dining Room should be repainted.

If much of the work in the house has been discreet, the Trust's approach outside has been less self-effacing. In the stable block a substantially new interior has been fitted within the eighteenth-century exterior to take a shop, education room, audio visual room and other reception facilities. The restaurant between the stables and the house is the one new building at Beningbrough. Designed by Martin Stancliffe on the site of some dilapidated greenhouses, it makes much use of materials salvaged from elsewhere at Beningbrough. There were many abandoned buildings which required work before Beningbrough could reopen; the Victorian laundry, for example, has been restored and the laundry courtyard cobbled. It is survivals such as these which have helped contribute to

Beningbrough's success since its reopening in 1979.

The reopening has not put an end to the work of improvement at the house. The Blue Bedroom was opened in 1981 to house a second splendid state bed, purchased for the Trust the previous year by the National Art-Collections Fund. In 1982 several rooms, including the Hall and the Saloon, were double-hung by the National Portrait Gallery to present a richer display. Conservation work continues: the Trust has recently had the great carved cartouche above the garden entrance to the house conserved in its statuary conservation workshop at Cliveden, while the National Portrait Gallery has begun a programme of cleaning the Kit-cat portraits in the Dining Room.

What of the future? Here so much depends on funds. A glimpse of life 'below stairs' in the basement, modest though it is, would be an antidote to the glories above. Archaeological investigation of the sites of the Elizabethan house and the early eighteenth-century stables could provide welcome additional information on the history of Beningbrough. Even replanting the large walled kitchen garden would be possible, if sufficient money could be found. But the most important task has been achieved: the future of the house is secure, and Beningbrough now gives pleasure to more people than at any time in its long history.

### NOTES

1 Sale held by Curtis & Henson on the premises, 10–13 June 1958.

2 National Trust Registry file 2264/M (Box 1205 F6).

3 John Garrett, 'Beningbrough Restored', *National Trust Magazine*, Spring 1979.

4 The others were Saltram (1957), Hardwick (1959), Dyrham (1961), Sudbury (1967) and Cragside (1977).

5 Much of the information in this chapter is drawn from National Trust files. Useful accounts of the restoration have been published by Binney and Stancliffe (see Bibliography). See also note 6 below.

6 Mlinaric discussed his work at Beningbrough in *Vogue*, August 1979, pp. 122–5. His career is charted by Ann Barr in *Tatler*, cclxxxv, April 1990, pp. 102–8, 152.

7 It has since been discovered that in 1894 the Hall floor was relaid (L.P. Dawnay's MS notebook, 1892–1910); a note discovered when the boards were taken up suggests that further work was done in 1922.

# CHAPTER FIVE

# THE PAINTINGS

When Beningbrough reopened to the public in 1979, it did so with a superb collection of English portraits from the National Portrait Gallery. These portraits – paintings, sculpture, pastels and engravings – form a history in miniature of national life from the time of the 'Glorious Revolution' in 1688, which signalled the end of the Stuart dynasty, up to and beyond the succession of George III as king in 1760, the first Hanoverian to speak English as his native language.

If these years were remarkable for witnessing Britain's rise to the position of a world power, they also saw the end of the traditionally dominant role of foreign artists in London. The long line of great names from the Continent – Holbein, Van Dyck, Lely, Kneller – was brought to an end with the rise to fame of Hogarth, Ramsay, Gainsborough and Reynolds. This chapter examines the development of English art from 1680 to 1760, and the studio practice of artists working at this time. But first, how did these paintings come to Beningbrough?

Three fine collections have filled the rooms at Beningbrough. Firstly, the Bourchier family collection, which was continued by the Dawnays until the house was sold in 1916. Next came the pictures from Holme Lacy in Herefordshire, brought by the 10th Earl of Chesterfield when he and his wife moved to Beningbrough; these remained until the

*(80) 'Stag Hunting in Galtres Forest'; in the manner of Jan Wyck (Saloon). This overdoor painting is one of the few surviving at Beningbrough from the Bourchier collection*

sale following Lady Chesterfield's death in 1957. Most recently, the present collection of paintings from the National Portrait Gallery, some 120 portraits of the late seventeenth and eighteenth centuries, arranged on all three floors at Beningbrough.

Of the Bourchier collection, twelve paintings remain in the house, mostly by virtue of their being fixed in the panelling as overdoors. In the Saloon two early eighteenth-century canvases, *Stag Hunting in Galtres Forest* (Nos 80, 84), remain while a pair by Jacob Bogdani of exotic birds, dated 1720, have gone, leaving the enfilade overdoors bare. Elsewhere on the ground and first floors are family portraits dating from between 1650 and 1760 (Nos 21, 24, 44, 50–1, 54, 86, 89). Most of these are rather uncertainly identified and the attributions should be treated with caution. The only signed paintings are those by John Verelst of 1699 in the State Bedchamber, perhaps representing the last Sir Barrington Bourchier and his wife (Nos 21, 24). But it would be a mistake to think of the family collection as including portraits only. The great landscape view of Beningbrough is reproduced on the cover of this guidebook. There were also a number of Grand Tour souvenirs, including paintings and sculpture collected in Italy by Margaret Bourchier and her husband Giles Earle in the 1770s. Their trophies included several views of Naples and a number of old masters of apparently indifferent quality which were sold in 1892. Fortunately their marble bust of Pope Clement XIV by Christopher Hewetson (No. 9) still remains at Beningbrough to dominate the entrance hall from the vantage point of the fireplace as visitors come in. Many of the early Bourchier and Earle portraits were sold at Christie's in the 1892 sale or in 1919, but others still belong to the Dawnay family.

From the Chesterfield era five family portraits remain, including the 10th Earl by F. E. Bertier (No. 95) and his wife by Ellis Roberts (No. 99), a society artist favoured by the family. Their collection included many Scudamore portraits, inherited from the Earl's grandfather; those that were not sold in the 1958 Beningbrough sale are now to be found at Kentchurch Court, Herefordshire.

By far the majority of the pictures in the house today are from the National Portrait Gallery, and as a result portraits of the famous predominate. As John Cornforth has aptly put it, 'the company now at Beningbrough is thus a much richer and more fascinating one than ever trundled up the avenue to see the Bourchiers in the 18th century'.

The portraits at Beningbrough have been chosen for their quality, national importance and local interest, and to match the period of the house. Thus Lord Carlisle and Vanbrugh, patron and architect at Castle Howard, thus also Thomas Ripley, the Yorkshire architect who walked to London to seek his fortune, Laurence Sterne of Shandy Hall and John Carr of York.

*(8) George I; by Sir Godfrey Kneller, 1716 (Hall)*

## PORTRAIT PAINTING FROM KNELLER TO REYNOLDS

In 1716, the year Beningbrough was completed, George I's portrait was painted by Sir Godfrey Kneller, court painter to four monarchs from William III. This coronation portrait (No. 8) now surmounts the Hall fireplace at Beningbrough and shows the King in the robes of a Knight of the Garter, with the crown, orb and sceptre to his side. The previous year had seen the crushing of the Jacobite revolt in Scotland, led by the 'Old Pretender', Prince James Stuart, son of King James II. It was the Hanoverian George I and not Prince James who had succeeded Queen Anne, the last of the Stuart monarchs, in 1714. By the Act of Settlement in 1701, Parliament had ruled that only a Protestant could take the throne. George I, or Georg Ludwig as he had been christened, spoke no English and had never been to England before becoming king at the age of 54 in 1714. But he was Protestant and he was a great-grandson of James I.

Like George I, Godfrey Kneller (1646/9–1723) was both Protestant and German. He was not yet 30 when he arrived in London in 1676. Over the course of almost fifty years he stood at the centre of British culture and his shadow was to fall heavily on his successors. Experienced and cosmopolitan – he trained in Holland under Bol and perhaps Rembrandt, and also studied in Rome and Venice – Kneller found in London that the business of painting was completely dominated by the demand for portraits.

Kneller gained his entrée to court circles through the Duke of Monmouth's secretary, James Vernon, whose portrait at Beningbrough (No. 11) was one of the very first he painted in England. Kneller's attitude to Vernon was one of self-interest, as a letter written to his brother in April 1677 makes clear: 'I am doing the portrait of the secretary of the Duke of Monmouth... The secretary will pay me like a courteous gentleman, and I shall treat him so that he will be my friend; he can introduce me to courtiers, for I take him for an honest and most charming gentleman.' Vernon did indeed introduce Kneller to the Duke and helped him rent a fine suite of rooms close to Whitehall.

Though Monmouth, the illegitimate son of

*(11) James Vernon; by Sir Godfrey Kneller, 1677 (Smoking Room)*

Charles II, lost his life in 1685 in his attempt to claim the throne from his uncle, James II, Kneller was by then well established at court. When William and Mary came to the throne three years later, Kneller was appointed Principal Painter, a post he was to hold for 35 years. At first this commission was held jointly with the English-born John Riley, but then in sole capacity following Riley's death in 1691. Kneller was knighted by the King the following year, thus reinforcing his position. He became the chosen painter of the dominant Whig faction, and many of the King's ministers and supporters turned to him for their portraits: witness his three paintings of the 1690s at Beningbrough of the Duke of Bedford, the Earl of Halifax and the MP Thomas Papillon (Nos 2, 55, 52).

The finest of Kneller's later works are his portraits of the Kit-cat Club, of which 20 are at Beningbrough (Nos 25–42, 116, 138), and as many again at the National Portrait Gallery. The club's interests coincided with Kneller's own: to uphold the 'Glorious Revolution' and the Protestant succession.

*(34) Richard Lumley, 2nd Earl of Scarborough; by Sir Godfrey Kneller, 1717 (Dining Room)*

Founded in the last years of William III, largely by Somers, the Lord Chancellor, and the publisher Jacob Tonson, its secretary, the club began meeting in Christopher Cat's tavern near Temple Bar in London, and took its name from his mutton pies, known as 'Kit-cats'. Its influential membership included leading Whig MPs and landowners, soldiers like Essex and Stanhope, the writers Addison, Vanbrugh and Walsh, as well as Marlborough and Burlington, though these last two are missing, not having descended with the set from Tonson.

By 1715, with the French defeated, George I on the throne and the first Jacobite rising repelled, the objectives of the club were achieved, and by 1725 Vanbrugh was writing to Tonson about the club as a memory, and expressing a wish to have one meeting that winter, 'not as a club, but old friends that have been of a club, and the best club that ever met!'

The portraits were gifts from members to Tonson, and were painted by Kneller over a space of more than twenty years. He adopted a standard 'kit-cat' format of 36 × 28 inches, rather larger than the more usual 30 × 25 inches; the larger size readily allowed one of the sitter's hands to be shown and encouraged a wider variety of poses. They were framed as a set for two guineas each by the framemaker Gerard Johnson, in 1733, probably at the time Tonson's nephew built a special room to house the pictures at his home at Barn Elms in Surrey. The set was made known to a much wider audience through the collection of mezzotints of the portraits, engraved by John Faber and published in 1735, a group of which are displayed in the State Dressing Room at Beningbrough.

Of Kneller's rivals, the work of John Closterman (1660–1711), German-born like Kneller but French-trained, is represented at Beningbrough by two of his greatest achievements, the elegant *Taylor Family* and the more severe double-portrait, *Lord Shaftesbury and his brother* (Nos 81, 83). Following the death of his former partner, John Riley, in 1691, Closterman's reputation grew, perhaps owing to the showiness and richness of his best work. In 1698 he travelled to the Continent and from Rome wrote to his patron, the 3rd Earl of Shaftesbury, who was one of the most influential philosophical writers of his time. With Shaftesbury to guide and inspire him, Closterman produced some of his finest work, and his patron has left a vivid sketch of 'my painter [Closterman]' in the heat of artistic creation 'going in to his picture when in the dark and standing long before it'. Shaftesbury's portrait at Beningbrough, probably painted on Closterman's return to London, is one of the most extraordinary of its era and a precursor of the Neo-classical style. It was surely planned by the sitter to reflect his opinions on portraiture and, as explained on p. 72, to symbolise his viewpoint as a Neoplatonist.

When Kneller died in 1723, there was no natural successor. Richardson, Jervas and Vanderbank each had their following but they lacked Kneller's stature. The oldest of this new generation was Jonathan Richardson (1665–1745). A pupil of Riley, he painted in a solid unpretentious style best suited to portraits of men. Two late works at Beningbrough are his self-portrait and that of the celebrated court physician, Dr Richard Mead (Nos 137,

141). By contrast, the Irish-born Charles Jervas (c.1675–1739) excelled with women's portraits. He was a pupil of Kneller, whom he succeeded as Principal Painter to the King, but this appointment was no guarantee of success. The coronation portrait of George II (No. 5) is a studio version of the full-length commissioned by the City of London for the Guildhall in 1727. As a painting it is worthy but dull, and his almost contemporary portrait of the King's seven-year-old son, the Duke of Cum-

berland, is no better (No. 113). So it is hardly surprising to read in a slightly later account in 1732 that 'Mr Jervase . . . has had no success in painting their Majesties pictures & from thence he lost much favour & Interest at Court'. Jervas's earlier fame had come from his portraits of writers, including Richard Steele and Jonathan Swift. At Beningbrough his intriguing full-length of Alexander Pope (No. 49), who at one time was so friendly with the artist as to take painting lessons from him, may have

*(83) Anthony Ashley-Cooper, 3rd Earl of Shaftesbury and his brother, the Hon. Maurice Ashley-Cooper; by John Closterman, c.1700–1? (Saloon)*

*(7) Frederick, Prince of Wales; by Philip Mercier, c.1736 (Hall)*

been painted at the poet's direction, to show him musing on the trial of strength facing him in his impending translation of Homer's *Iliad*, which was published between 1715 and 1720.

If the King chose to be painted by Jervas, it was typical of the Hanoverians that the Prince of Wales should turn elsewhere. Prince Frederick appointed the German-born Philip Mercier (1689/91–1760) as his Principal Portrait Painter in 1729, and from his hand is the handsome three-quarter-length of the Prince (No. 7) dating to the mid-1730s. Mercier knew the work of the French rococo painter Watteau well and was instrumental in bringing something of his lightness of touch and colour to England. When he finally lost the Prince's favour he moved to York where he was the best painter to take up residence there in the eighteenth century. From 1739 to 1751 he supplied a stream of attractive portraits to almost all the great houses of Yorkshire, including Beningbrough (his charming full-length of the four-year-old Mildred Bourchier still belongs to the Dawnay family).

It is easy to forget how many painters worked in provincial centres outside London during the eighteenth century. William Hoare (c.1707–99) painted the portraits of numerous fashionable visitors to Bath between 1738 and 1780, including Alexander Pope, Christopher Anstey and Lord Chesterfield (Nos 104, 132, 96). George Beare (fl.1743–9) worked at Salisbury during the 1740s, painting portraits for local worthies such as Francis Price (No. 125) with a directness worthy of Hogarth. George and John Smith of Chichester (1713–76 and 1717–64), known for their landscapes and still-lives, are represented at Beningbrough by a self-portrait group (No. 45). Even Thomas Gainsborough (1727–88) began his career outside London, preferring to spend long periods at Ipswich, where he painted portraits of Joseph Gibbs the composer and Admiral Vernon (Nos 92 and 93, both of the 1750s) and at Bath (the portrait of Stringer Lawrence, No. 74, belongs to about 1774, the year he left Bath for London).

London was ever a rich target for foreign artists. Of those represented at Beningbrough, Pieter Angellis (1685–1734) (see No. 48) came from Antwerp in about 1716, and over the next five years he was followed by Giuseppe Grisoni (1699–1769) from Rome, Balthasar Denner (1685–1749) from Hamburg and Herman van der Mijn (1684–1741) and his son Frans (1719–83) from Antwerp (see Nos 114, 46, 23, 115). However, the only visitor who posed a significant threat to the increasing dominance of British-born artists was Jean Baptiste van Loo (1684–1745), who arrived from Paris in 1737 (see No. 70). He attracted such a spate of fashionable sitters that the engraver George Vertue could note that 'the English painters have had great uneasiness; it has much blemished their reputation and business'. But his vogue was short-lived and in 1740 the young Allan Ramsay (1713–84) was writing complacently, 'I have put all your Vanloos and Soldis and Ruscas to flight and now play the first fiddle myself'. Following van Loo's departure the jingoistic feelings caused by the outbreak of war with France in 1741 put a stop to the influx of foreigners and gave a younger generation of British artists their chance. The most fiercely patriotic of these was William Hogarth (1697–1764), who even took

*(58) John Montagu, 4th Earl of Sandwich; by Joseph Highmore, 1740 (Blue Bedroom)*

to signing some of his work as 'W. Hogarth *Anglus*'. In his portraits of the 1740s he broke away from earlier small-scale conversation-pieces. His grand full-length of Captain Coram, a gift to the Foundling Hospital, London, in 1740, was painted to stake his claim to a leading position in his profession.

Ramsay was premature in claiming the part of 'first fiddle'. Two other artists prominent in the 1740s, Joseph Highmore and Thomas Hudson, are well represented at Beningbrough, and Hudson in particular dominated the London market. Highmore (1692–1780), the older man by almost ten years, was a sensitive portrait painter who displayed a Hogarthian directness in his best work. For his friend the novelist Samuel Richardson (see No. 133), he painted a charming series of illustrations to his novel *Pamela*, engraved in 1745. Highmore's other two portraits at Beningbrough, *Lord Sandwich* (No. 58) and *Thomas Ripley* (No. 69), also belong to the 1740s, which was perhaps his most successful decade. The one is a haughty image of the young nobleman in Turkish costume just returned from the Grand Tour, while the second is painted in a rather softer manner to show the ageing architect against a background of a little classical rotunda.

Though to modern eyes Highmore's poses and settings are more inventive than those of his younger rival, it was Thomas Hudson (1701–79) who took the lion's share of fashionable portraiture in the 1740s. Hudson provided a safe, undemanding product, witness his early canvas of the German composer J. C. Pepusch (No. 135) or the much later painting of Lord Egmont (No. 134), both rather stiff costume-pieces. However, his finest portraits, such as those of Susannah Cibber (No. 47) and Sir Peter Warren (No. 63), both painted in a showy style full of colour and surface attraction, make it easier to understand his great vogue. For a time his only real rival was Ramsay, represented at Beningbrough by the delicate portrait of Robert Wood (No. 130). But by the mid-1750s his pupil, Joshua Reynolds (1723–92), recently returned from Italy, was making severe inroads into his business. One need look only at Reynolds's portraits of James McArdell (No. 112) and William Chambers (No. 128), both of the 1750s, to see how the younger artist abandoned the much-repeated formulae of the past to breathe a sense of life and feel of spontaneity into his sitters. 'The exuberance of his invention', Horace Walpole wrote, 'will be the grammar of future painters of the portrait.' Throughout his career, Reynolds continued to conjure up new ways to present his sitters in their portraits, often using the Old Masters as a source of inspiration. It was this ability to innovate which led Gainsborough to make his famous comment on Reynolds, 'Damn him! How various he is!'

THE PRACTICE OF PORTRAIT PAINTING

It was Reynolds who gave the practice of painting a new respectability as a profession rather than a trade or vocation. The first painter to be knighted since Kneller in the 1690s and the founding president of the Royal Academy, Reynolds delivered an annual discourse to the assembled academicians and students in which he put forward a theoretical and academic basis for the art of painting.

The foundation of the Royal Academy and with

*(38) Charles Mohun, 4th Baron Mohun; by Sir Godfrey Kneller, c.1707 (Dining Room)*

*(66) William Pulteney,*
*1st Earl of Bath; by*
*Sir Joshua Reynolds, 1761*
*(Great Staircase)*

it the Academy Schools in 1768 marked the beginning of the end of the well-established tradition of studio training. Reynolds and Joseph Wright of Derby had both trained under Hudson, Hudson and George Knapton under Richardson, Richardson under Riley and Riley under Gerard Soest. As a result there is a strong consistency in practice throughout the period. It is worth looking more closely at the two men who dominated their profession, though half-a-century apart: Kneller and Reynolds.

Kneller's practice is not well documented, but an examination of some of the many paintings by the artist at Beningbrough is revealing. His method was always to begin with the head, as he told Alexander Pope, indicating the body only in quick outline. This can be seen very clearly in mezzotints of three unfinished Kit-cat portraits – Shannon, Walsh and Huntingdon (State Dressing Room) – and also in his less typical triple head of Lord Nottingham (No. 101), which is really a finished work in itself and perhaps intended as a guide for a sculptor to work from. Kneller was known for the speed at which he worked. 'He painted with an amazing quickness, without any appearance of study, and often times at the first stroke', reported André Rouquet, a Swiss visitor to London. The very rapid, almost transparent quality of his paint, full of fluidity and quite oily in character, can be seen at its best in some of his Kit-cat portraits such as those of Godolphin (No. 42) and Mohun (No. 38), where the range of flesh tones is limited, the furrows of the brushstrokes are readily distinguishable and the cold grey ground is left exposed around some of the facial features and in the voluminous wigs.

'Kneller was in every respect a different pattern to

follow; and yet all English painters would fain imitate him, would fain adopt his manner', Rouquet lamented. 'Several were so affected as not to cover the whole canvas, that is in those parts where its tint and its colour might answer the purpose, because Sir Godfrey Kneller had done so.' Something of this can be seen in Bartholomew Dandridge's *William Kent* (No. 145).

Later in the century Gainsborough was to call Kneller to his defence when writing to a client who had complained about the 'roughness of surface' in his portrait: 'Sir Godfrey Kneller used to tell them that pictures were not made to smell of; and what made his pictures most valuable with the connoisseurs was pencil or touch.' But by this time Kneller's reputation was in eclipse.

We know more about Reynolds. On his return from Italy in 1752 he brought with him Giuseppe Marchi, who became the first member of his studio and stayed with him for almost his entire career. Others followed, so much so that Joseph Farington in his memoirs of Reynolds could say that his school 'resembled a manufactory, in which the young men who were sent to him for tuition were chiefly occupied in copying portraits, or assisting in draperies, and preparing backgrounds'. James Northcote's letters from his five years as a student-assistant to Reynolds in the 1770s confirm this impression, but he conceded of Reynolds that 'the whole together of the picture, was at last his own, ... his own slight and masterly work was still the best'.

At Beningbrough Reynolds's portrait of William Pulteney, Earl of Bath (No. 66) is a superb image of the celebrated orator in old age. How it was painted and what Lord Bath thought of his portrait are revealed in the extensive correspondence between him and the blue-stocking Mrs Elizabeth Montagu who requested the portrait as a mark of respect and friendship for Lord Bath. Sittings took place on 28 and 31 August, 17 September, 16 October and 30 December 1761. To begin with Mrs Montagu was enthusiastic about the portrait, writing to a friend on 6 September, 'it will be very like him but not so handsome, as long as he lives I shall look on it with pleasure, always with reverence'. Lord Bath had remarkably penetrating and brilliant eyes, noted by

Mrs Montagu, and one of the faults she later found with the painting was in this feature. So on 30 December Bath returned to the studio: 'On Wenesday... I will most certainly be at Mr Reynolds' to mend my sickly looks. ... I fear they will not be much mended by any Physick of Mr. Reynolds. He has made an old man look as if he was in pain, which an old man generally is, and so far he is right.'

But it is an earlier letter, written on 15 October, which provides an unusual insight into the common practice of employing a specialist drapery painter:

I have discovered a secret by being often at Mr. Reynolds, that I fancy he is sorry I should know. I find that none of these great Painters finish any of their Pictures themselves. The same Person, (but who he is, I know not) works for Ramsay, Reynolds, & another, called Hudson, my Picture will not come from that Person till Thursday night, and on Fryday it will be totally finished, and ready to send home.

That 'Person' could well have been Peter Toms (fl. 1748–77), a pupil of Hudson, who is said to have painted the draperies for the great full-length of

*(47) Susannah Cibber; by Thomas Hudson, 1740s (Drawing Room)*

Lady Elizabeth Keppel (Woburn Abbey, Bedfordshire), which was going through Reynolds's studio at precisely the same period as Bath's portrait.

Such a practice was not new. Thomas Hudson had been employing a drapery painter since at least the early 1740s and indeed it was in Hudson's studio at this time that Reynolds learned the tricks of the trade. It is said that what precipitated the break between Reynolds and his master was when he had to carry a painting through the rain for the drapery painter, Joseph van Aken (c.1699–1749), to finish.

Although specialist assistants had been common in large studios for centuries, the practice of employing an independent sub-contractor to finish part of the painting was seldom as highly developed as in the London market of the mid-eighteenth century. It became common knowledge that van Aken, a Flemish painter who had come to London in the early 1720s, worked for Ramsay, Hudson and others. When van Aken died in 1749, Hogarth published a caricature 'composed of all the portrait painters of the metropolis as mourners, and overwhelmed with the deepest distress'. Almost certainly the draperies in Hudson's portrait of the actress Susannah Cibber (No. 47) are by van Aken, whose rather shiny silks and satins with their deliberate folds are easy to recognise. It is less easy to identify the hands at work in Hudson's later portraits but his *Lord Egmont* (No. 134) was probably finished by an assistant or drapery painter.

This practice was already well established in the seventeenth century. John Closterman acted as John Riley's drapery painter for a time in the 1680s, the two artists dividing the proceeds equally for larger portraits, and later he himself employed Jacques Parmentier (1658–1730), who was wont to refer scornfully to portrait painters as 'phiz-mongers'. Such an unusual picture as *Lord Shaftesbury and his brother* (No. 83) is probably entirely from Closterman's own hand, but in his *Taylor Family* (No. 81) the flowers at least are likely to be the work of a specialist painter.

A few independent spirits, most notably Hogarth and for a time Gainsborough, avoided using studio assistants altogether. But the painting of portraits was not well paid and to grow rich as Kneller did meant having a full appointment diary – Kneller

*(85) Georgiana Spencer, later Duchess of Devonshire; by Sir Joshua Reynolds, c.1761 (Lady Chesterfield's Room)*

had as many as fourteen sittings in a day, or so he claimed – and a well-organised studio to assist with the more routine parts of the work.

In general eighteenth-century portrait painters did not make much use of preparatory drawings or oil sketches. An interesting exception is the portrait of Miss Georgiana Spencer (No. 85) at the age of four, the Duchess of Devonshire to be. It is a sketch probably made at a single sitting for the portrait with her mother, Lady Spencer (at Althorp in Northamptonshire), and is entirely by Reynolds. On 12 September 1761 (coincidentally the very month when Lord Bath was sitting for his portrait), Lady Spencer attended Reynolds's studio at eight o'clock in the morning for her fourth and last sitting while her daughter was entered in the diary for one o'clock the same day. Reynolds rarely made sketches or drawings, but there are a number of vivid oils of young children whom he has tried to catch in a single sitting. In this case his efforts were rewarded, for the finished portrait at Althorp is one of the artist's supreme achievements.

# CHAPTER SIX

# THE CHINA CLOSETS

The fashion for incorporating 'china closets' into country houses was still at its height in 1716, when Beningbrough was completed. The house retains six of these small rooms, with their original corner chimney-pieces surmounted by stepped shelves, for the display of Chinese and Japanese porcelain. The secret of producing this beautiful and useful material was not to be discovered in the West until 1709, and throughout the seventeenth century and much of the eighteenth century 'china-mania' was to grip the rich and powerful throughout most of northern Europe.

Until the end of the sixteenth century, porcelain was rare in Europe, apart from in Portugal and Spain. It was often mounted in silver and used as a royal gift to be displayed in a curiosity cabinet. This fashion persisted in France, Germany and Italy until the middle of the seventeenth century, but in Holland the formation of the Dutch East India Company in 1602 brought more immediate changes. In the same year the Company captured the Portuguese carrack *St Iago* off St Helena and subsequently auctioned its cargo of Chinese porcelain at Middelburg. Dutch trade with China grew enormously during the first half of the seventeenth century, until the turmoil caused by the overthrow of the native Ming rulers by the Manchus in the 1640s virtually stopped the export of porcelain from China. For the next thirty years the Dutch turned to the Japanese potters in the southern province of Arita to make good the deficiency. The Chinese came back into contention in the early 1680s after kilns were re-established at Jingdezhen, and by the middle of the eighteenth century they had virtually destroyed Japanese competition by selling a whiter and thinner porcelain for considerably less. At the same time the almost complete Dutch monopoly of the trade had disappeared with the advent of the British East India Company, which dominated the export of oriental porcelain for the rest of the eighteenth century.

The first European to have made a *porzellan-*

*An engraving by J.-B. Broebes of the famous seventeenth-century porcelain room in the Oranienburg Palace, near Berlin, published in 1773*

*kabinett*, or china closet, was the Princesse Luise Henriette of Orange, the wife of the Elector Friedrich Wilhelm I of Brandenburg-Prussia. Between 1652 and her death in 1667 she amassed a sizeable collection of porcelain, which was displayed in the Oranienburg Palace, near Berlin. The cabinet was later dismantled and the contents redisplayed by her son Friedrich in an extraordinary Baroque room whose walls were covered from floor to ceiling in porcelain. After he became the first King of Prussia in 1701, Friedrich built the Palace of Charlottenburg (completed in 1706), west of Berlin, with its own mirror porcelain cabinet. Large sheets of mirror-glass were often set into the walls of such cabinets to enhance the lustre and exaggerate the sheer profusion of porcelain plates, dishes and other pieces, placed on tiers of brackets around the room. The result was a spectacular decorative ensemble, in which Chinese and Japanese pieces were mixed without regard for their origin. An example still exists at Schloss Weissenstein, at Pommersfelden, built in 1719.

The craze for porcelain was equally strong in France. By 1681 Louis XIV owned 1,004 pieces of

*The chimney-piece in the south-west Closet is decorated in the traditional manner with early eighteenth-century 'famille verte' Chinese porcelain on loan from the Ashmolean Museum, Oxford*

*Blue-and-white Chinese porcelain in Lady Chesterfield's Dressing Room*

porcelain, according to inventories of his collection. Another inventory made for the Dauphin in 1689 lists 381 pieces, mainly blue-and-white, of which 194 formed the 'Garniture de cheminée de la chambre de Monseigneur'.

It was probably through Queen Mary and Holland that the fashion reached England in the late seventeenth century. (The fact that the 1677, 1679 and 1683 inventories of the closets at Ham House in Surrey mention no porcelain lends support to this theory.) In 1687 the German architect Nicodemus Tessin visited Queen Mary's country house, Huns-slardiek, near the Hague, where the chimney-piece in the Audience Chamber was 'full of precious porcelain, part standing half inside it, and so fitted together that one piece supported another'. Daniel Marot, the Huguenot architect and designer, may

have been responsible for this arrangement. He left France for Holland in 1684, and is also believed to have been consulted by Christopher Wren in the redesigning of the Water-Gallery at Hampton Court. It was described by Celia Fiennes as 'decked with China and fine pictures of the Court Ladyes drawn by Nellor; beyond this came severall roomes and one was pretty large, at the four corners were little rooms like closets or drawing roomes one panelled all with Jappan another with looking Glass and two with fine work under pannells of glass.' It is likely that much of the porcelain was removed to Kensington Palace where Queen Mary appears to have already placed some of her porcelain. An inventory taken by Simon de Brienne, Keeper of His Majesty's Wardrobe, in 1696/7, gives details of where the porcelain stood in the Gallery at Kensing-ton Palace – 19 pieces over each of the chimneys, seven to nine pieces over each of the doors, others put on the floor under tables or on pedestals, but large amounts put on top of lacquer and other cabinets, as one can see today at Ham House. Sometimes several pieces were joined together: 'Two stands each stand made up with three jarrs & one china platt at the top.' A similar piece can be seen in the Ante-Library at Belton House in Lincolnshire, where a vase $30\frac{1}{4}$ inches high is composed of a Kangxi blue-and-white triple-gourd sprinkler, on top of a Japanese Arita vase, which itself is on a Kangxi ginger jar.

The fashion for china closets remained popular throughout the first half of the eighteenth century; designs for a porcelain gallery in the Japanese Palace at Dresden were made as late as 1735. Rooms were also created to display European porcelain, the first being constructed at Brunn for Count Dubsky's Vienna porcelain, c.1730. Similar displays were popular in Italy and Spain. One of the last was in the Royal Palace at Madrid, a Neo-classical room made of Buen Retiro porcelain between 1770 and 1780. Elsewhere in Europe, porcelain rooms fell out of fashion in the later eighteenth century and were mostly dismantled. Macaulay in his *History of England* attacked Queen Mary's taste, complaining that 'almost every great house in the Kingdom maintained a museum of these grotesque baubles'.

With the opening up of China to westerners after

the Opium Wars of the 1840s and '50s, interest in Chinese porcelain revived. Perhaps the greatest scholar of this period was Stephen Bushell (1844–1908), who went to China in 1868 as physician to the British Legation in Peking. He wrote *Oriental Ceramic Art* in 1896, which contains a mass of vital information virtually impossible to find elsewhere. His granddaughter, Dorothy Bushell, donated more than sixty pieces from his collection to the National Trust, many of which are now housed at Beningbrough. Of a later generation was Gerald Reitlinger (1900–78), whose collection at Wood-gate House, near Beckley in Sussex, was massed as densely as its seventeenth- and eighteenth-century predecessors. According to Richard de la Mare there

*This 1906 'Country Life' photograph shows the Closet chimney-piece when the Dawnay family's china was still in the house*

were 260 pieces of Chinese blue-and-white in Reitlinger's spare bedroom alone. He gave his collection to the Ashmolean Museum in Oxford, which has kindly loaned more than twenty pieces to Beningbrough.

An inventory of the china in the house in January 1909, still in the possession of the Dawnay family, together with the photographs taken by *Country Life* at about the same date, suggest that Beningbrough probably followed a classic evolution of taste. Excluding pantries and storerooms, some 800 pieces of porcelain were scattered in 27 rooms and corridors. About half the porcelain was Chinese blue-and-white and *famille verte* as well as Japanese Imari, similar to that which is now in the house and which may originally have been displayed in the china closets. The other half of the inventory shows that in the late 1750s the family had probably acquired a large quantity of Chelsea dessert wares similar to those in the factory's 1755 sale catalogue. Other purchases of both decorative and useful china seem to have been made throughout the nineteenth century, so that by 1909 there were pieces placed in almost every conceivable corner of the house.

When, in the 1970s, the National Trust sought to restore the interior of Beningbrough to its early eighteenth-century appearance, it used the evidence of old inventories and of those china closets still in existence as a guide in arranging porcelain on the stepped shelves of the corner chimney-pieces. Plates and dishes were hung on the walls of the Dressing Room closet in a manner evocative of earlier china closets. The well-known eighteenth-century practice of putting large vases on the hearth was also followed. (The 1710 inventory of Dyrham Park in Gloucestershire records 'a large Pyramid Delf Flower pot in ye chimney', both in the Vestibule and the Best Bed Chamber.) The result is a modest, but vivid reminder of the passion for porcelain that swept Europe in the seventeenth and early eighteenth centuries.

# CHAPTER SEVEN

# TOUR OF THE HOUSE

## THE HALL

The front door opens immediately into the Hall, which rises through two storeys, introducing a note of monumentality and a Baroque interest in spatial effect which is carried on throughout the house. In the eighteenth century this room would have been the hub of everyday life, with servants passing to and fro and waiting visitors sitting on the Hall chairs. On occasions the room would also have been used for large celebratory banquets. In the nineteenth century it took on the air of an informal drawing-room, but it was furnished once again as a hall after the Chesterfields purchased the house in 1917.

### DECORATION

The purely architectural character of the room is closely paralleled by those at Castle Howard and Bramham – both Yorkshire houses where Thornton is known to have worked.

Giant fluted pilasters of the Composite order stand on high plinths round the walls and support a very individual form of groined vault – almost Gothic in character – which probably derives from De Rossi's engravings of Borromini's church of the Collegio di Propaganda Fide in Rome. The splaying of the central first-floor window reveals accentuates the perspective in typically Baroque fashion. The plasterwork is restrained but of fine quality, especially in the elaborate keystones to the arches and windows. These support large wall panels resembling church tablets, and are flanked by bold acanthus leaves with chains of husks issuing from the mouths of grotesque masks, somewhat in the manner of Hawksmoor's detail at Easton Neston in Northamptonshire. To judge by their shallow relief, it is possible that the recessed wall panels were originally intended to be painted in *trompe-l'oeil*, as with Pellegrini's decoration at Castle Howard. On Thornton's death in 1721, a York plasterer called John Bagnall was one of his two executors, and

Bagnall may well have been responsible for the plasterwork at Beningbrough.

Above each of the four doors in the side walls are magnificent wrought-iron grilles, attributed to the famous Derbyshire blacksmith Robert Bakewell, who supplied nearly identical ironwork for St Anne's, Manchester, in 1712. Presumably they would have arrived at Beningbrough by boat, having been brought up the Trent and the Ouse.

The evolution of the Hall during the twentieth century is recorded in a series of photographs. A 1906 article in *Country Life* shows a gallery running across the Hall at first-floor level linking the two sides of the house, which was probably inserted around the 1830s. It was removed after the Chesterfields purchased the house in 1917. At the same time the two round-headed arches at the south end of the Hall were filled in to match the doorcases at the other end of the room. Originally, they would have been open to the transverse corridors on each side, providing a splendid vista down the centre of the house. The doors themselves are all of mahogany, probably replacing earlier walnut ones.

The present decorative scheme is the fourth this century. The Dawnays painted the room uniformly white, but the Chesterfields marbled the pilasters and chimney-piece and sage-tinted the walls; they were subsequently painted cream. By the late 1970s this was looking shabby and the Trust decided to reintroduce a Baroque scheme. The plinths were stripped of later layers of paint and found to be of solid York stone, as at Castle Howard. This provided the key to the current scheme. The pilasters were painted a creamy stone colour to harmonise with the plinths, and shades of grey were used for the wall areas behind. The ironwork panels were repainted dark green, a colour found under many later layers. The redecoration was completed with the replacement of the wooden floor by stone flags, matching the originals in the adjacent staircase hall and corridors – all made possible through the generosity of an anonymous donor.

*The Hall*

*The Hall in 1906,
before the first-floor
gallery was removed*

### CHIMNEY-PIECE

In the centre of the west (right-hand) wall the massive stone chimney-piece has a curved pediment with enriched keyblock and console brackets.

### PICTURES

In each room they should be viewed clockwise from the entrance door. On the ground floor the display commences with the royal portraits in the Hall and continues very roughly chronologically: the 1688 Revolution (Smoking Room), the Kit-cat Club (Dining Room) through to the mid-eighteenth century.

1 *John Churchill, 1st Duke of Marlborough (1650–1722) and Colonel John Armstrong (1674–1742)*
By an unknown artist, partly after Sir GODFREY KNELLER (1646/9–1723)
Queen Anne's Commander-in-Chief and the future 'Chief Engineer of England' planning the siege of Bouchain (1711). NPG 5318

2 *William Russell, 1st Duke of Bedford* (1613–1700)
Sir GODFREY KNELLER (1646/9–1723), signed,
*c*.1692
Liberal nobleman who worked to achieve and then
preserve the Revolution Settlement of 1689. He is
depicted in his robes as Knight of the Garter.

NPG 298

3 *Queen Anne* (1665–1714) *as Princess of Denmark
with her son, the Duke of Gloucester* (1689–1700)
After Sir GODFREY KNELLER (1646/9–1723),
*c*.1694
The future queen (reigned 1702–14) is shown with
the only one of her seventeen children to survive
infancy. Her son's death at the age of eleven
compelled Parliament to look to Hanover for an
heir to the throne.

NPG 325

4 *Augusta, Princess of Wales* (1719–72)
CHARLES PHILIPS (1708–47), signed, *c*.1736
Daughter of Frederick II of Saxe-Gotha; married
Frederick, Prince of Wales in 1736.

NPG 2093

5 *George II* (1683–1760)
Studio of CHARLES JERVAS (*c*.1675–1739), *c*.1728
The last British sovereign to command in the field,
at the Battle of Dettingen, in 1743. A version of the
coronation portrait, with Westminster Abbey in the
background.

NPG 368

6 *Prince George of Denmark* (1653–1708)
By or after MICHAEL DAHL (1656/9–1743), *c*.1705
Easy-going consort of Queen Anne, whom he
married in 1683. Lord High Admiral.

NPG 4163

7 *Frederick, Prince of Wales* (1707–51)
PHILIP MERCIER (1689/91–1760), signed, *c*.1736
Son and political opponent of George II, and father
of George III; patron of Mercier, whom he appointed his Principal Painter.

NPG 2501

8 *George I* (1660–1727)
Sir GODFREY KNELLER (1646/9–1723), signed,
1716
Came to the throne in 1714, thus safeguarding the
Protestant Succession. Elector of Hanover. A ver-
sion of the coronation portrait.

NPG 5174

## SCULPTURE

9 *Pope Clement XIV* (1705–74)
CHRISTOPHER HEWETSON (1739–99), signed,
Rome, 1771
Marble bust
Lorenzo Ganganelli, Pope 1769–74, best known for
his suppression of the Jesuit Order. The bust was

probably acquired by Giles and Margaret Earle
during their lengthy stay in Italy in the 1770s, and
has been at Beningbrough ever since.

## FURNITURE

A mid-eighteenth-century high-backed hall chair
with the arms of Sir Edwyn Francis Scudamore-
Stanhope, grandfather of the 10th Earl of Chesterfield. Chesterfield collection.
Three replica hall chairs, without the armorial
bearings, made by Dick Reid of York, 1980.
Three reproduction hall tables, based on a model at
Dunham Massey, Cheshire, made by Dick Reid,
1980.
Nineteenth-century box grate and steel serpentine
fender with pierced rail. Dawnay collection.

## CERAMICS

Two Chinese blue-and-white chargers, mid-eighteenth-century.

# THE SMOKING ROOM

The absence of early inventories of the house
prevents us from knowing the original purpose of
this room. However, its masculine character with
Doric frieze, and its position immediately adjoining
the Hall, suggest that it may originally have been a
business room. It has been known by its present
name since at least the turn of the century.

## DECORATION

Here the visitor is introduced to the richly carved
woodwork which is a feature of so many of the
interiors at Beningbrough. The cornice is made up
of bold Doric triglyphs giving a highly architectural
feeling to the room. The model for this unusual
feature, which can also be found at another of
Thornton's Yorkshire commissions, Wentworth
Castle, is probably an engraving by William III's
French architect, Daniel Marot, published in Am-
sterdam about 1700. The doorcases and two overmantel frames, the lower one presumably intended
for a small mirror or 'landskip glass', are also
beautifully carved.
    A 1906 photograph shows the room painted in
white, which was the prevailing tone of the house
during the Dawnay ownership. It was repainted a
fashionable bluey-green colour in the 1930s. The

rich red-brown of the present paint was introduced in 1978 and is based on a colour found in the house (under many later layers) and paralleled in other houses of the same date.

### CHIMNEY-PIECE

The fireplace is one of a number introduced by the Dawnays in the 1830s.

### PICTURES AND SCULPTURE

10 *The Seven Bishops Committed to the Tower in 1688*
ENGLISH, *c.*1688
The bishops opposed James II's pro-Catholic religious policy: on their release from the Tower they were acclaimed as heroes. NPG 79

11 *James Vernon* (1646–1727)
Sir GODFREY KNELLER (1646/9–1723), 1677
Tried to reconcile Charles II with his illegitimate son, the Duke of Monmouth, and later became a staunch Whig and a confidant of William III. This is one of Kneller's first paintings of an English sitter. NPG 2963

12 *Dr Samuel Clarke* (1675–1729)
JAMÉ VERHYCH, signed, 1719
Lead bust
Divine, and metaphysical philosopher; his treatise on the Trinity, 1712, excited much controversy. NPG 4838

13 *William III* (1650–1702)
? DUTCH, *c.*1690
William of Orange reigned with Mary, the elder daughter of James II, from 1688. Seen here at the Battle of the Boyne, 1690. NPG 1026

14 *Samuel Pepys* (1633–1703)
Attributed to JOHN CLOSTERMAN (1660–1711), *c.*1690–1700
Diarist; a brilliant naval administrator, he held the post of Secretary of the Admiralty until his enforced retirement at the 1688 Revolution. NPG 2100

### FURNITURE

A Boulle *bureau Mazarin* of ebony inlaid with brass, late seventeenth-century. Chesterfield collection.
A late seventeenth-century Chinese coromandel screen reduced to five panels. (The remainder are in the Dining Room and the south-west Dressing Room.) Mrs P. Tritton loan.

Three carved walnut side chairs with cane seats and backs, late seventeenth-century. Megaw bequest.
Chinese export lacquer cabinet on stand with later brass knobs, eighteenth-century. On loan from the Castle Museum, York.

### CERAMICS

Chinese Imari plate, *c.*1730. Fox bequest.
Two English plates copying a Chinese Imari design, early nineteenth-century. Fox bequest.
Lamp, made from an early eighteenth-century Kangxi jar.
Japanese apothecary jar with almost contemporary Dutch decoration in Imari and European styles, early eighteenth-century.
Oriental baluster jar and cover, nineteenth-century. Fox bequest.
Chinese jar with *Sang-de-boeuf* glaze, nineteenth-century. Bushell bequest.

### CARPET

Persian Herez rug, *c.*1920.

# THE GROUND-FLOOR CORRIDORS

As you leave the Smoking Room, one of the most remarkable features of the design of Beningbrough becomes apparent: the way in which a corridor stretches through the centre of the house from east to west, offering a vista from one end of the building to the other. The great attention which was paid to the design of circulation spaces in Baroque houses reflects the important part which procession still played in the formal life of the upper classes in the early eighteenth century. Food was served with great ceremony, and guests would pay visits to the apartments of their hosts and other guests according to a rigid protocol.

### DECORATION

As in other Baroque houses, the architecture of the corridors is treated as an extension of the Hall, whose restrained colour scheme they share. The corridors, almost certainly inspired by those at Castle Howard, comprise a series of linked but distinctly treated spaces. At each end of the house there is a Doric pilastered lobby, square at the west end and rectangular at the east. Moving inwards there is a domed lobby in the west and a groin-vaulted lobby in the east. The latter is based on Borromini's church of the Propaganda Fide in Rome. All cornices, doorcases, brackets and pilasters are of carved wood rather than plaster, demonstrating the skill of William Thornton's team of carvers.

The view along the corridor is best seen from the east end where the chamfering inwards of the mouldings below the arches creates an illusion of exaggerated perspective along the passageway. The vista would have been all the more impressive before the arched openings into the Hall were filled in with doors.

### PICTURE

15 *James II* (1633–1701)
? FRENCH, *c*.1690?
Reigned 1685–8; his rule threatened the return of despotism and Catholicism, and he fled to France as 'Dutch William' entered London.      NPG 366

### FURNITURE

Oak chest for storing clothes with a decorative frieze inscribed 'MH 1735'.

# The State Apartment

As was the usual practice in English houses of this period, the chief bedchambers were to be found on the ground floor, served by small closets or 'cabinet' rooms at the corners of the main block. These suites of rooms were described collectively as an apartment and the grandest of them – known as state apartments – usually included an ante-room or withdrawing room of the kind that once occupied the eastern half of the Drawing Room (see below). Their use was closely related to the strict protocol and etiquette of the Baroque period. They were intended not merely for sleeping, but also for ceremonial visits by other guests, interviews and

*The State Dressing Room. The alignment of the ground-floor doors provides a view along the whole length of the south front*

even dealing with staff. Each room in the sequence of an apartment was more exclusive than the last, and compliments to or from a visitor could be measured both by how far one was invited along the sequence, and by how far the occupant of the apartment came along it to meet you. The bed-chamber and withdrawing room were therefore surprisingly public, and smaller, more private 'cabinet' rooms were provided at the end of the sequence.

# THE STATE CLOSET AND DRESSING ROOM

To ease circulation, visitors see the most private room of the apartment, the Closet, first. The cupboard on the inside wall housed the close stool containing a chamber-pot. But such a room was not purely utilitarian. Together with the adjacent Dressing Room, the two rooms would have made up for their size by the richness of their original decoration, generally containing the best small pictures, wall-hangings of velvet or damask, or a mass of porcelain, as in some of Daniel Marot's engravings. Here the occupant of the apartment would read, write, or receive their closest friends.

## DECORATION

Both rooms are panelled in pine with elaborately carved entablatures and overdoors in various soft-woods. The detail of the door surround in the Dressing Room is comparable to Thornton's sur-viving work at Bramham. The pine would origin-ally have been painted, but was stripped by Lord and Lady Chesterfield in the 1920s.

## CHIMNEY-PIECES

The Bourchiers evidently shared Queen Mary's overwhelming passion for china, for all four sets of Dressing Rooms and Closets at Beningbrough have chimney-pieces with stepped ledges set across the corner in the manner introduced by Christopher Wren at Kensington Palace and Hampton Court. These were specially designed for Delftware and oriental pieces imported by the English and Dutch East India companies in increasing quantities from the late seventeenth century. Besides the scope they gave for displaying porcelain, corner chimney-pieces had great practical advantages in enabling up

to four rooms to share the same flue. The fire surrounds of both rooms are of Derbyshire fossil marble of the type used by the Smiths of Warwick in many of their houses in the Midlands at about this time. Francis and William Smith also kept a well-known stoneyard and could easily have retailed marble to other provincial architects such as William Thornton. The cast-iron hob grate in the Closet was installed in the 1830s, while that in the Dressing Room is a Carron & Co. grate of the late eighteenth century.

## CERAMICS

Mostly Chinese Kangxi blue-and-white porcelain, early eighteenth-century. Fox and Bushell bequests. Loans from the Ashmolean and Victoria & Albert museums, and the Lady Lever Art Gallery. (Further details available from the Room Stewards.)

## THE STATE CLOSET

### FURNITURE

English walnut reading table with adjustable top, early eighteenth-century. Megaw bequest.
Queen Anne walnut wing armchair with 'shep-herd's crook' arms and *gros point* needlework seat. Megaw bequest.

## THE STATE DRESSING ROOM

### PICTURES

16 *George Legge, 1st Baron Dartmouth* (1648–91)
After JOHN RILEY (1646–91), *c*.1690
Admiral; given command of the fleet in 1688 by James II, a personal friend, but failed to intercept William III.                                    NPG 664

17–18 *William III* (1650–1702) *and Mary II* (1662–94)
Engravings by P. VAN GUNST after J. H. BRANDON, published at The Hague                         NPG

Also exhibited are mezzotint engravings of the Kit-cat Club by JOHN FABER after Kneller; many of the original pictures are displayed in the Dining Room.

### FURNITURE

English walnut secretaire on bun feet, *c*.1700. Megaw bequest.

Walnut stool, early eighteenth-century with later alterations. Megaw bequest.
Two Dutch chairs with raked backs, *c*.1700. Chesterfield collection.
Octagonal walnut candlestand with barley-twist stem, late seventeenth-century.

# THE STATE BEDCHAMBER

This room was created as the second best bedchamber in the house, perhaps for use by the owner, John Bourchier. The original state bedchamber, reserved for the most distinguished guests, was situated in what is now the western half of the Drawing Room.

### DECORATION

The bedchamber was invariably the most richly decorated and furnished of the rooms of an apartment. Here the frieze is an outstanding display of the York carvers' skills; luxuriant acanthus leaves form a continuous scrolling pattern, framing at intervals on the east and west walls four beautifully sculptured masks representing the Seasons. The carved overdoors have superbly ornate surrounds and are so similar to some at Wentworth Castle that they must be by the same hand. The frames for the missing 'landskip glass' and overmantel above it are also carved in extraordinarily high relief, with a three-dimensional quality rarely found in the work of contemporary craftsmen outside London. The door to the Dining Room, blocked either in Lady Chesterfield's day or earlier, has recently been reopened and now gives a splendid vista down the whole enfilade of the state rooms along the south front, a characteristic feature of the planning of Baroque houses.

### CHIMNEY-PIECE

An original bolection-moulded fire surround of Derbyshire fossil marble.

### PICTURES

19 *John Locke* (1632–1704)
JOHN GREENHILL (1644?–76), *c*.1672–6
'Who, best of all Philosophers, understood the Powers of the human Mind, . . . and Bounds of Civil Government; and . . . refuted usurped Authority.'
NPG 3912

*The carving in the Drawing Room is among the finest in the house*

20 *John Dryden* (1631–1700)
Attributed to JAMES MAUBERT (1666–1746), *c*.1695
Dramatist and Poet Laureate, an office he lost at the 1688 Revolution. A late portrait, symbolic of the poet's inspiration and genius. NPG 1133

OVERDOOR:

21 *?Sir Barrington Bourchier* (1672–1700)
JOHN VERELST (fl.1697–1734), signed, 1699
Knighted 1697; half-brother of the builder of Beningbrough.

22 *William Congreve* (1670–1729)
Studio of Sir GODFREY KNELLER (1646/9–1723), *c*.1709
Yorkshireman; the greatest English master of the comedy of manners. NPG 67

23 *James Brydges, 1st Duke of Chandos* (1674–1744)
HERMAN VAN DER MIJN (1684–1741), *c*.1721–5
Paymaster-General to the Duke of Marlborough, and vastly rich in consequence. Patron of the arts, for whose chapel at Cannons Handel wrote the Chandos Anthems. This is the surviving part of a double portrait of the Duke sitting to his wife for his portrait.                                    NPG 530

OVERDOOR:

24 *?Mary Bourchier* (d.1700)
JOHN VERELST (fl.1697–1734), signed, 1699
Wife of Sir Barrington Bourchier (No. 21).

### STATE BED

Beningbrough was built at a time when the art of upholstery in England was at its height. Through the influence of Huguenot craftsmen, state beds took the form of vast confections of velvet, damask and silk, edged with gold and silver braid and trimmed with bows, rosettes and tassles. As the focal point of a state apartment, huge sums were spent on such beds, with curtains, wall-hangings, chairs and stools frequently upholstered *en suite*. The cost was often more than all the other contents of the house put together. This crimson damask state bed originally came from Holme Lacy in Herefordshire. It was brought to Beningbrough by Lady Chesterfield in

*Detail of the richly upholstered state bed from Holme Lacy (State Bedchamber)*

about 1918, and acquired by the Treasury at the sale after her death in 1957. It is one of the finest Baroque state beds, in the style of Daniel Marot, to survive in England.

In the centre of the elaborately fringed and braided backboard is a Viscount's coronet, probably that of the 2nd Viscount Scudamore who succeeded in 1697, and who, in 1710, married a daughter of Lord Digby. The maker of the bed is not known, but it may well be the work of Francis Lapierre, the leading Huguenot upholsterer in London at this time, who made similar 'angel tester' beds for the Duke of Devonshire and for William III. A particularly rare feature are the two pelmet boards above the windows which match the sides of the bed tester and must have been made *en suite*. The bed was restored by Morant & Co. before 1909, and much of the damask has had to be replaced, then and more recently.

### FURNITURE

Early eighteenth-century red Japanned longcase clock. The movement is by Edmund Breckell, London. Chesterfield collection.
Late seventeenth-century French Louis XIV armchair, embroidered with *petit* and *gros point* needlework. Ullstein loan.
Walnut chest-on-stand with 'oyster' veneer, late seventeenth-century.
Walnut stool with turned legs and tapestry cover, late seventeenth-century. Megaw bequest.
Walnut candlestand with barley-twist stem, late seventeenth-century. Megaw bequest.
Two similar, but not identical, looking glasses with Vauxhall plates and gilt gesso frames in the manner of Gumley and Moore, early eighteenth-century. Megaw bequest.
Pair of William and Mary walnut side chairs. The carved crestings match the front stretchers. Megaw bequest.
A William and Mary walnut side table with 'oyster' veneer top and unusual elm legs. Megaw bequest.
Walnut candlestand with barley-twist stem, late seventeenth-century. Megaw bequest.

### CERAMICS

Two Chinese vases with Wucai (five colour) decoration, late transitional Ming-Qing dynasty, *c*.1660.
Chinese *famille rose* punchbowl, Qianlong, *c*.1780.
Chinese *famille rose* bowl, late eighteenth-century.

*The Dining Room*

English carpet, possibly Exeter, copying a Persian design.

## THE DINING ROOM

At first probably called 'the Parlour', it originally functioned as a kind of inner hall, giving access to the garden and providing a subdued start to the gradual climax of ostentation in the sequence of state rooms to either side. It probably became a dining-room at some time during the nineteenth century, when the opening to the State Bedchamber was blocked and that door moved to the opposite corner of the room. This has now been returned to its original position, necessitating some rearrangement of the pine panelling.

### DECORATION

The comparative plainness of the decoration, befitting its original function, is more austere than that of the adjoining rooms. It depends for effect on the architectural qualities of the deep bolection panelling and correctly classical entablature with its modillioned cornice. Unusually, the doors to the Hall and the garden face each other to one side of the

room rather than in the centre. Symmetry was impossible, as the south-west State Apartment contained one more room (now subsumed within the Drawing Room) than the flanking apartment in the south-east corner.

Paint analysis suggests that the room was originally decorated in white, but the Chesterfields grained the panelling to resemble walnut and picked out Thornton's carving in gold. The room has now been redecorated using an appropriately masculine grey-green colour, found at Boughton House in Northamptonshire and other late seventeenth-century houses and considered an ideal background for the double-banked Kit-cat portraits in their original early eighteenth-century gilt frames.

### CHIMNEY-PIECE

The present marble chimney-piece with its egg-and-shell surround was introduced by the Chesterfields, and was apparently copied from that in the Blue Bedroom. It replaced a Grecian marble one of the 1830s. The overmantel, with its splendidly carved brackets and pedimented picture frame, is probably original to the room. It is similar in form to one at Castle Howard, but has a more Palladian feel than most of the rest of Thornton's work at Beningbrough.

PICTURES

The Kit-cat Club (Nos 25–42)

By Sir GODFREY KNELLER (1646/9–1723)
Apart from Marlborough (No. 43), whose portrait in the series is missing, all the portraits in this room were painted by Sir Godfrey Kneller for the Kit-cat Club, a celebrated group of Whig writers and politicians. They were pledged to the Protestant succession and to the defeat of Louis XIV.

The Club first met at the tavern kept by Christopher Cat near Temple Bar. It took its name from his mutton pies, known as 'Kit-cats'. These portraits, in matching frames, painted by Kneller between c.1697 and 1721, were given to the NPG through the National Art-Collections Fund in 1945, and are now divided between London and Beningbrough. They are more fully discussed above on p.35. Two more from the set are on the second floor.

25 *Charles Dartiquenave* (1664–1737), 1702
Epicure and wit; 'the man who knows everything, and that everybody knows'.        NPG 3201

26 *James Stanhope, 1st Earl Stanhope* (1673–1721), c.1710
Soldier, diplomat, politician and scholar. Commander of the British forces in Spain until his capture at Brihuega (1710); chief minister of the Whig government, with special responsibility for foreign affairs, under George I.        NPG 3225

27 *Charles Cornwallis, 4th Baron Cornwallis* (1675–1722), c.1705
Politician.        NPG 3200

28 *John Montagu, 2nd Duke of Montagu* (1690–1749), 1709
Courtier and eccentric; known for his bizarre acts of charity and his love of practical jokes.        NPG 3219

29 *Charles Sackville, 6th Earl of Dorset* (1638–1706), c.1697
Poet and patron of poets; publicly supported the Seven Bishops (see No. 10, Smoking Room); he holds a white wand of office as Lord Chamberlain to William III.        NPG 3204

30 *John Dormer* (1669–1719), c.1715
Country gentleman; Deputy Lieutenant of Oxfordshire, 1701.        NPG 3203

31 *Thomas Hopkins* (d.1720), 1715
Money-lender, especially to the nobility. NPG 3212

*(32) Charles Montagu, 1st Duke of Manchester; by Sir Godfrey Kneller, c.1712*

32 *Charles Montagu, 1st Duke of Manchester* (1662–1722), c.1712
A pillar of the Revolution of 1688 and a highly successful diplomat.        NPG 3216

33 *Charles Lennox, 1st Duke of Richmond and Lennox* (1672–1723), c.1703
Son of Charles II and the Duchess of Portsmouth; deserted the exiled James II in France to make his career in England.        NPG 3221

34 *Richard Lumley, 2nd Earl of Scarborough* (1688?–1740), 1717
Soldier; Master of the Horse to George II.
NPG 3222

35 *John Tidcomb* (1642–1713), c.1710
Soldier; served in Portugal.        NPG 3229

36 *William Walsh* (1663–1708), c.1708
Poet and critic; friend of Alexander Pope. Left unfinished at Walsh's death; only the head is by Kneller.        NPG 3232

37 *Edmund Dunch* (1657–1719), c.1705
MP, wit and gamester; Master of the Household to Queen Anne; married Elizabeth Godfrey, a mem-

ber of the Marlborough family and a toast of the Kit-cat Club.    NPG 3206

38 *Charles Mohun, 4th Baron Mohun* (1677–1712), *c.*1707
Soldier and notorious duellist; twice tried for murder by the House of Lords before he was twenty years old; he holds a snuff-box inset with an unidentified miniature.    NPG 3218

39 *Abraham Stanyan* (1669?–1732), *c.*1711?
Secretary to the British Ambassador in Paris; from 1705 envoy to Switzerland, of whose government he published an account in 1714.    NPG 3226

40 *John Vaughan, 3rd Earl of Carbery* (1639–1713), *c.*1708
Pepys called him 'one of the lewdest fellows of the age'; firmly supported the Revolution of 1688; a patron of Dryden.    NPG 3196

41 *Algernon Capel, 2nd Earl of Essex* (1670–1710), *c.*1705
General; served in all William III's campaigns.    NPG 3207

42 *Francis Godolphin, 2nd Earl of Godolphin* (1678–1766), *c.*1712
Son of Queen Anne's first minister, and himself a politician; married a daughter of his close ally, the Duke of Marlborough.    NPG 3209

OVERMANTEL:

43 *John Churchill, 1st Duke of Marlborough* (1650–1722)
Attributed to JOHN CLOSTERMAN (1660–1711), after JOHN RILEY (1646–91), *c.*1685–90
General; defeated the armies of Louis XIV, most signally at the Battle of Blenheim in 1704, after which the huge palace erected for him by a grateful Queen Anne was named.    NPG 501

### FURNITURE

Nine dining chairs (from two different sets) with vase-shaped splat backs and cabriole legs, decorated on the legs with finely carved lion and satyr masks. In the style of Giles Grendey, *c.*1735. Lady Lever Art Gallery loan.
Oak gate-leg table, with oval top and turned legs, *c.*1660. Cooper-Abbs bequest.
Chinese coromandel screen of five panels, the remainder in the Smoking Room and south-west Dressing Room, late seventeenth-century. Mrs P. Tritton loan.

### CERAMICS

Two Chinese Wucai beakers. Late transitional Ming-Qing dynasty, *c.*1660.

### CARPET

Twentieth-century Persian carpet, possibly from the Sultanabad region.

# THE DRAWING ROOM

This was originally two smaller rooms divided by a wall down the centre, the eastern section being the withdrawing room and the western the bed-chamber of the State Apartment. The excellence of the carving by Thornton and his team of carvers in the deep cornices, overmantels and overdoors reflects the importance of this set of rooms. In the Baroque period the State Apartment symbolised the status and power of the particular family or individual. Landowners had to be prepared for receiving guests of equal or higher rank than themselves in befitting style.

During the nineteenth century the dividing wall was taken down. It was probably done in the 1830s as part of a scheme of improvements by the 6th Viscount Downe soon after he inherited. This was a period when the creation of large reception rooms on the ground floor was fashionable, and at Sudbury Hall in Derbyshire, Salvin created a similar room out of the old Drawing Room and Library.

### DECORATION

Although the two halves of the room today have very different entablatures, their common use of bolection-moulded panelling has minimised the disharmony. The extraordinary quality of the carving in the western half is almost the equal of Grinling Gibbons in its dexterity. The frieze consists of a series of tapering plinths (a device also found at Gilling Castle in Yorkshire), which support projecting portions of the lower member of the cornice. In the frieze, shells, supported by palm fronds, are surmounted alternately by vases and by the monogram JMB, standing for the builder of the house John Bourchier and his wife Mary. The monogram appears again, flanked by eagles' heads, in the cresting of the overmantel.

The frieze of the eastern section has as its theme pairs of large acanthus brackets with pierced scroll

59

*The Drawing Room*

tops, somewhat similar to the paired consoles supporting the cornice on the outside of the house. A similar frieze recurs at Wentworth Castle, in the room known as 'Queen Anne's Sitting Room', where William Thornton and his team are known to have worked. The panels above the doors at each end of the room, carved with vases of flowers resting on lambrequins, and with doves nestling in the acanthus scrolls each side, are also close to some at Wentworth Castle, and betray the influence of Jean Berain or his chief pupil, the Huguenot Daniel Marot. A collection of Berain's arabesque designs, engraved by Dolivar, was published in 1693, and Marot's several different series of ornamental designs, issued in a complete edition as his *Oeuvres* in 1700, would also have been available to English craftsmen of the following decade. The fact that Thornton's colleagues, Jean Godier and Daniel

Hervé, were Huguenot refugees may well have influenced this York team of craftsmen in their choice of pattern-books.

When the two rooms were thrown into one, some juggling round of the carved work was necessary. The two facing doorcases at each end are a pair and probably came from the western half (the Bedchamber), while the door on the inside wall has sadly lost its pair and is probably from the eastern (Withdrawing Room) section. The fluted vases above the facing overdoors closely resemble the vases in the frieze of the western half and, although the single door has a shell under the portrait which also matches those in the same frieze, it looks like a later insertion. Originally, there seems to have been no door from either of the rooms to the Great Staircase.

In addition to these alterations, after 1917 Lady Chesterfield had much of the panelling re-set or renewed, and exchanged the more elaborate overmantel carving over the chimney-piece now in the western half with the simple rectangular pattern (centering once again in a shell) now in the eastern. However, it seems possible that she was merely restoring the original arrangement, as the over-mantel now in the western half includes the monogram JMB, which is repeated in the frieze, and the floral carving closely resembles that of the door surround adjacent to it. Lady Chesterfield also had the room stripped of paint in the fashion of the day. Though this was done with great skill, it exposed the disparate natural colours of the pine wood used by the carvers, something not originally intended to be revealed.

## CHIMNEY-PIECES

The two chimney-pieces with their green marbled, bolection-moulded surrounds were introduced by the Chesterfields. That in the west wall had previously been of Grecian design and was presumably introduced in the 1830s. The chimney in the north end had originally been in the cross-wall, but was presumably moved to its present position when the room was knocked into one.

*(46) George Frideric Handel; by Balthasar Denner, c.1726–8*

## PICTURES

44 *?Mary Bellwood, Mrs John Bourchier* (1683–1746)
Attributed to JONATHAN RICHARDSON (1665–1745), *c.*1720
Wife of the builder of Beningbrough.

45 *George and John Smith* (1713–76 and 1717–64)
SELF-PORTRAITS, *c.*1760
Landscape painters; the standing figure is probably George Smith, the most gifted of the three brothers known as 'the Smiths of Chichester'.  NPG 4117

46 *George Frideric Handel* (1685–1759)
BALTHASAR DENNER (1685–1749), *c.*1726–8
Composer; in 1711 settled in England, to which he introduced the oratorio; his *Messiah* was first performed in 1742.  NPG 1976

47 *Susannah Maria Cibber (née Arne)* (1714–66)
THOMAS HUDSON (1701–79), 1740s
Actress and singer – the contralto arias in Handel's *Messiah* were written for her; sister of the composer Thomas Arne, and briefly married to the play-wright Colley Cibber's disreputable son, Theophilus.  NPG 4526

48 *Queen Anne and the Knights of the Garter*
PIETER ANGELLIS (1685–1734), signed, 1720s?
Perhaps the Chapter of the Order of the Garter held at Kensington Palace on 4 August 1713, at which six new knights were installed.  NPG 624

49 *Alexander Pope* (1688–1744)
CHARLES JERVAS (*c.*1675–1739), *c.*1715
Poet; painted by his close friend, Jervas, when he was just beginning his translation of Homer, and perhaps portraying the conflicting demands of fame, as represented by the bust of Homer, top left, and friendship, signified by the female figure, sometimes identified with Pope's friend, Martha Blount.  NPG 112

OVERDOOR:

50 *?Judith English, Lady Dolben* (*c.*1731–71)
ENGLISH, *c.*1750
Said to be the wife of Sir William Dolben, 3rd Bart, and daughter and heir of Somerset English, House-keeper of Hampton Court.

OVERDOOR:

51 *?Elizabeth Mackworth*
ENGLISH, *c.*1700
Said to be the wife of Henry Mackworth, but no such person is traceable.

52 *Thomas Papillon* (1623–1703)
Sir GODFREY KNELLER (1646/9–1723), signed,
1698
East India merchant; MP for Dover, 1673–95.
NPG 5188

53 *?Dorothy Walpole, Lady Townshend* (1686–
1726)
Studio of CHARLES JERVAS (c.1675–1739), c.1715
In Turkish dress; sister of Sir Robert Walpole and
wife of the 2nd Viscount Townshend.   NPG 2506

OVERDOOR:

54 *?John Bourchier* (1684–1736)
Attributed to JONATHAN RICHARDSON (1665–
1745), c.1720
The builder of Beningbrough.

*Late seventeenth-century English walnut pier-glass and
matching pier-table in the Drawing Room. The dish is early
eighteenth-century Chinese 'famille rose'*

### FURNITURE

A pair of English walnut pier-tables with 'seaweed'
marquetry and 'oyster' veneer, double-scroll legs
and X-shaped stretchers in the manner of Gerrit
Jensen, c.1690. Chesterfield collection. Jensen was
cabinetmaker to the royal household during four
reigns from Charles II to Queen Anne. Presumably
Flemish or Dutch by birth, he had settled in London
by 1680.
A pair of walnut pier-glasses with bevelled plates
and elaborate pierced crestings. *En suite* with the
tables, c.1690. Chesterfield collection.
Longcase clock with movement by Thomas Ogden
of Halifax (1693–1769).
Gilded overmantel (landskip) glass, c.1725. Megaw
bequest.
Walnut oval gate-leg table with deep frieze, late
seventeenth-century. Megaw bequest.
A set of seven mahogany armchairs and a sofa, in the
Chinese style with blind fretwork decoration,
c.1760. From Coleshill, Berkshire.
Queen Anne walnut 'oyster' veneer bureau book-
case with broken segmental pediment, mirror-glass
panels and unusually elaborate chased brass fittings.
Megaw bequest.
Square piano in mahogany case by John Preston,
The Strand, London, c.1780. W.J.Craig gift.
Walnut stool of cabriole legs with needlework
upholstery, c.1725. Megaw bequest.
Chinese lacquer screen of eight panels, eighteenth-
century.
Regency mahogany dining table with column
support and acanthus decoration. Chesterfield col-
lection.

Coromandel workbox, nineteenth-century.
Cooper-Abbs bequest.
French giltwood console table with elaborately
carved apron and stretcher, and Brescia marble top,
c.1740. Chesterfield collection.
Louis XV bracket clock with Boulle and ormolu
case. The movement is by Tallon of Paris. Chesterfield collection.
A pair of bronze figures of Venus and Hercules.

### CERAMICS

Two Chinese *famille rose* chargers. Qianlong, mid-
eighteenth-century.
Lamp, made from Chinese *famille verte* baluster jar.
Kangxi, early eighteenth-century. Bushell bequest.

Lamp, made from Chinese Wucai beaker vase. Transitional period, *c.*1660. Bushell bequest.
Chinese *famille verte* dish. Kangxi, early eighteenth-century. Ashmolean Museum loan.

### CARPETS

A large Persian Feraghan carpet in the 'guli henna' design on a blue field with 'turtle' border, twentieth-century.
A Persian runner, probably Bidjar, late nineteenth- or early twentieth-century.

# THE DRESSING ROOM AND CLOSET

These two small rooms with their corner chimney-pieces correspond to the pair already seen at the other end of the south front, and were intended to serve the adjacent State Bedchamber.

### DECORATION

Like their counterparts, both are wainscotted with bolection-moulded panels. The overmantels, with

*The Dressing Room*

stepped ledges, were again especially designed for the display of porcelain, and the Closet has a cupboard on the inside wall intended for the close stool. These rooms would originally have been richly decorated, and the lacquered and japanned furniture reflects that taste for the exotic which the imports of the East India companies were encouraging on an ever increasing scale. 'Cabinet rooms' at Drayton in Northamptonshire and Honington in Warwickshire are decorated with sections of Chinese coromandel screens, cut up and inset in the panelling. In the fashion of the day the pine was stripped by the Chesterfields in the 1920s.

### CHIMNEY-PIECES

In both the Dressing Room and Closet the fireplaces have contemporary marble surrounds, but with later Carron & Co. cast-iron hob grates. The chimney-pieces are divided into three sections: a rectangular plain panel above the fireplace with a finely carved cornice, a narrow fielded panel above and the whole surmounted by a cupola form. That in the Dressing Room terminates in a gadrooned finial.

## THE DRESSING ROOM

### PICTURE

55 *Charles Montagu, 1st Earl of Halifax* (1661–1715)
Sir GODFREY KNELLER (1646/9–1723), *c*.1690–5
Introduced the Bill establishing the Bank of England; reformed the coinage.                    NPG 800

### FURNITURE

Gilt mirror or 'sconce' with bevelled plate in the style of Gumley and Moore, *c*.1720. The candlearms are later. Megaw bequest.
Queen Anne walnut knee-hole desk, *c*.1710. Megaw bequest.
Walnut side chair with vase-shaped splat back, cabriole legs and carved shell knees, early eighteenth-century. Megaw bequest.
Chased-brass lantern clock, the mechanism by Peter Closon, London, early seventeenth-century. Megaw bequest.
Two end panels from the coromandel screens in the Dining and Smoking Rooms. Mrs P. Tritton loan.
Pair of English japanned side chairs with vase-shaped splat backs and cabriole legs, early eighteenth-century. Megaw bequest.
Chinese export lacquer cabinet-on-stand, eighteenth-century.
Mahogany tripod pole-screen with *gros point* needlework panel, *c*.1760. Megaw bequest.

### CERAMICS

Chinese *famille verte* dish, Kangxi, *c*.1670. Ashmolean loan.
Chinese *famille rose* fish bowl, nineteenth-century. Ashmolean loan.

ON CHIMNEY-PIECE:

Collection of Chinese *famille verte* porcelain, Kangxi, early eighteenth-century. Ashmolean loan. (Room stewards have further details.)

ON HEARTH:

Two Chinese Wucai (five colour) jars, *c*.1660. Bushell bequest.

## THE CLOSET

### PICTURE

56 *George II and Figures associated with the Moravian Church*
Attributed to JOHANN VALENTIN HAIDT (1700–80), *c*.1752–4
Possibly painted to commemorate the passing of a Bill in 1749 exempting the Moravian colonists in America from taking oaths or bearing arms. Perhaps showing, at right, a nobleman handing news of the passing of the Act to Count Nicholas von Zinzendorf, missionary and leader of the Moravian Brotherhood.                    NPG 1356

### FURNITURE

Queen Anne walnut chest of drawers with fold-over top, original brass handles and key escutcheons. Megaw bequest.
Queen Anne walnut box with brass corner mounts. Megaw bequest.
Queen Anne walnut chair with cabriole legs and stuffed back and seat, covered in contemporary needlework. Megaw bequest.
Walnut candlestand with barley-twist stem and three splayed feet, *c*.1700. Megaw bequest.

CERAMICS

Chinese blue-and-white Kangxi bowl, c.1700.

ON CHIMNEY-PIECE:

Collection of Chinese *famille verte* porcelain, Kangxi, early eighteenth-century. Ashmolean loan.

ON FINIAL:

Facetted Wucai vase, Wanli, late sixteenth-century.

(Room stewards have further details.)

# THE CONSERVATORY

Attached to the west wall of the house is a late nineteenth-century conservatory supplied by Richardsons of Darlington. The need to control humidity in the house restricts the range of plants that can be grown, but predominantly cool-coloured species have been chosen for their scent and foliage. They include rhododendron, *Plectranthus* and *Sparmannia*.

# THE BLUE BEDROOM

The original function of this room is unclear. By the 1890s it had become a billiard room, and in the 1920s the Chesterfields used it as a study. It was furnished as a bedroom in 1980, when the Trust acquired the state bed.

## DECORATION

Occupying a less important position on the colder north side of the house, this is a comparatively sombre room with its bolection-moulded panelling of painted pine and simple moulded entablature. It is in marked contrast to the ornately embellished rooms on the south front.

## CHIMNEY-PIECE

In the centre of the east wall, the fireplace has a marble surround with egg-and-shell enrichment. The grate is mid-eighteenth-century, with an older fireback inscribed 'Pax' and dated 1679, presumably a reference to the peace treaty of Nijmegen signed that year.

## STATE BED

Queen Anne tester bedstead, attributed to Francis Lapierre and identical to the one in the State Bedchamber. It was probably also made for Holme

Lacy, but sold by the Chesterfields when they moved to Beningbrough in 1917. The modern damask hangings may have been copied from the original blue upholstery. Given to the National Trust by the NACF in memory of Guy Baron Ash of Wingfield Castle, Suffolk.

## PICTURES

57 *John Law* (1671–1729)
Attributed to ALEXIS-SIMON BELLE (1674–1734), c.1715–20?
Financier and speculator, whose schemes precipitated a financial crash in France in 1720.   NPG 191

58 *John Montagu, 4th Earl of Sandwich* (1718–92)
JOSEPH HIGHMORE (1692–1780), signed, 1740
In Turkish dress; visited Turkey while on the Grand Tour. First Lord of the Admiralty. He gave his name to the sandwich, which he ate when gambling.   NPG 1977

59 *Philip Dormer Stanhope, 4th Earl of Chesterfield* (1694–1773)
GEORGE KNAPTON (1698–1778), signed, c.1745
Statesman and author of the famous *Letters* attempting to instil good breeding in his natural son.

60 *Called John Aislabie* (1670–1742)
ENGLISH, c.1720
Chancellor of the Exchequer; expelled from the House of Commons in 1721 when the South Sea Company's scheme to pay off the national debt failed (the South Sea Bubble); creator of the gardens at Studley Royal in Yorkshire.   NPG 1754

61 *Called Sarah Churchill, Duchess of Marlborough* (1660–1744)
MICHAEL DAHL (1656/9–1743), c.1695–1700
Confidante of Queen Anne and forceful wife of No. 43.   NPG 712

## TAPESTRY

Flemish tapestry depicting the story of Nausicaa and Ulysses, seventeenth-century. Chesterfield collection.

## FURNITURE

Walnut-framed looking glass with original bevelled plate, early eighteenth-century. Megaw bequest.
French Louis XIII walnut and ebony gate-leg table with turned column legs, c.1660. Ullstein loan.
Walnut armchair with 'shepherd's crook' arms, cabriole legs and *gros point* needlework upholstery, early eighteenth-century. Megaw bequest.

Queen Anne walnut tallboy with cabriole legs. Megaw bequest.

Queen Anne walnut wing armchair with cabriole legs and upholstered with a fragment of Mortlake tapestry. Megaw bequest.

Two Dutch chairs with raked backs, *c*.1700. Chesterfield collection.

William and Mary walnut candlestand with octagonal top and turned stem on three scrolled feet. Megaw bequest.

Two oak stools with cabriole legs and drop-in seats with *gros* and *petit point* needlework, early eighteenth-century.

### CERAMICS

Chinese *famille rose* dish, late eighteenth-century. Fox bequest.

Two Chinese Wucai vases, transitional period, *c*.1660. Ashmolean loan.

ON CHIMNEY-PIECE:

Chinese *famille rose* and *famille verte* dishes, bowls and a vase, early eighteenth-century. Ashmolean loan.

### CARPET

Twentieth-century Persian carpet from the Sultanabad region.

## THE GREAT STAIRCASE

Leaving the Blue Bedroom the visitor again enjoys a series of distinctly treated spaces along the corridor which runs through the centre of the house. A Doric pilastered lobby is succeeded by a domed one before arrival in the great stairwell, one of the most remarkable rooms in the house. It occupies a space almost as large as the adjacent Hall and twice that of the more modest back stair, which mirrors it on the east side of the Hall. Such an arrangement is very different from that which Vanbrugh devised at Blenheim and Castle Howard where an identical pair of narrow stairwells flank the hall. Such a grand staircase was needed to link the State Apartment on the ground floor and the Saloon above, which, as the principal room on the first floor, was used for large gatherings. Both honoured guests staying in the State Apartment and those invited to the house for parties would have proceeded formally up this staircase.

### DECORATION

The ceiling above the staircase with its groin-vaulted cove continues the arrangement of the Hall. The rather awkward way in which the tops of the upper windows are again cut off to allow for the ceiling, and the lower range is also cut to allow for the middle flight of stairs, is evidence of Thornton's limitations as an architect, or possibly of a change of plan during execution.

The plasterwork decoration in the staircase is somewhat puzzling: the cornice and the mouldings of the rib-vaults are obviously original, but the frames on the side walls, with acanthus cresting above them centering on shells and baskets of flowers, and, even more, the pierced *rocailles* above the keystones of the arches on the ground floor, look like additions of about 1730 at the earliest. It may be that John Bourchier's son, another John, found the treatment of the walls here too austere and had these extra adornments carried out, possibly by the Italian plasterer Giuseppe Cortese, whose style they resemble and whose work is common in this part of the world.

The pair of pedimented doorcases at the foot of the Staircase, and another pair at the foot of the back stairs, are nineteenth-century and one of the few Victorian alterations to the house. Originally, the two ground-floor bedchambers were intended to be approached only from the Dining Room and Withdrawing Room (now the eastern half of the Drawing Room) in the centre of the south front.

### STAIRCASE

The grand cantilevered staircase of three main flights, constructed entirely of oak and internally strengthened with wrought iron, is of outstanding workmanship. The shallow treads, no less than 7 feet wide, are all parquetried, and on the underside panelled with deeply carved bolection mouldings.

On the two half-landings are marquetry panels inlaid with the arms of John Bourchier and his wife, Mary Bellwood, their initials, the reef-knot, which was the Bourchier emblem, and the date 1716, providing a *terminus ante quem* for the completion of this masterly piece of work, and indeed a date for the building of the house.

The balustrade is, however, the most remarkable part of the whole staircase: the very thin, beautifully carved balusters are rather similar to those at the Treasurer's House in York (probably another of

*The Great Staircase*

Thornton's commissions about this time), but the panels of carving which punctuate them are unique, an extraordinary attempt to convey in carved wood the impression of delicate wrought-iron work. (For the Huguenot carvers who worked with Thornton see Chapter Two.)

## PICTURES

62 *Called Philip, 3rd Earl of Chesterfield with his wife, Lady Elizabeth Savile, their three children and a Nubian slave*
ENGLISH, *c.*1715–20
Lent by Barnsley Corporation.

63 *Sir Peter Warren* (1703–52)
THOMAS HUDSON (1701–79), *c.*1751
Admiral; took Louisbourg from the French, 1745.
His tomb in Westminster Abbey is by Roubiliac.
NPG 5158

64 *A Girl with a Mask*
ENGLISH, *c.*1750–60
On loan from the Greville collection, Polesden Lacey.

66 *William Pulteney, 1st Earl of Bath* (1684–1764)
Sir JOSHUA REYNOLDS (1723–92), 1761
Opponent of Sir Robert Walpole; a noted speaker in Parliament, he is wearing his parliamentary robes. See p. 42 above. See p. 42 above. NPG 337

## SCULPTURE

65 *Samuel Johnson* (1709–84)
EDWARD HODGES BAILY (1788–1867), signed, 1828, after JOSEPH NOLLEKENS (1737–1823), 1777
Marble bust
Author of the famous *Dictionary*; celebrated for his conversation and personality, as immortalised by Boswell. · NPG 996

67 *Sir Isaac Newton* (1642–1727)
EDWARD HODGES BAILY (1788–1867), signed, 1828, after LOUIS FRANÇOIS ROUBILIAC (1705?–62), 1751
Marble bust
Mathematician, scientist and philosopher; discovered the composition of light and the principle of gravity. His birthplace, Woolsthorpe Manor in Lincolnshire, is owned and shown by the National Trust. NPG 995

*Lionhead masks on the mid-eighteenth-century mahogany commode in the Great Staircase Hall*

68 *John Perceval, 1st Earl of Egmont* (1683–1748)
VINCENZO FELICI (fl.1701–7), signed, Rome, 1707
Marble bust
Politician and Irish patriot; a founder of the colony of Georgia, 1732. NPG 1956

## FURNITURE

English mahogany commode with later marble top, *c.*1750. Four graduated drawers and at the angles console brackets with acanthus decoration, lion-head masks and brass rings. Fine chased-brass escutcheons. Gift of Mrs Helena Hayward in memory of her husband.

## CERAMICS

Large Chinese blue-and-white baluster vase and cover, Kangxi, *c.*1690. In the 1720s Augustus the Strong of Saxony is supposed to have exchanged a regiment of dragoons with the King of Prussia for two such vases. Ashmolean loan.

# THE SECONDARY STAIRS

The visitor returns through the Hall to the second-ary staircase. Here, in typical Baroque fashion, the cantilevered treads are doubled up for emphasis. Originally, the stair would probably have been for everyday use by the family, linking the apartments on the ground and first floors. Until recently the stairs were disfigured by an ugly luggage-lift constructed in the narrow well, which darkened the whole area considerably. This has now been re-moved and the missing parts of the wrought-iron balustrade re-made, with a generous grant from the Ironmongers' Company, and again painted dark green to match the ironwork in the Hall.

*The first-floor corridor runs the entire length of the house and is broken only by the Hall. The wrought-iron grilles were probably made by the Derbyshire blacksmith Robert Bakewell*

At the head of the secondary stairs an upper corridor runs through the centre of the building, only interrupted by the upper parts of the hall. As on the ground floor the passageway comprises a series of distinct architectural spaces with, on this east side, a groin-vaulted lobby leading to a rectangular Ionic pilastered area with surmounting roundels and an enriched cornice. The acanthus decoration to the door surrounds is of the highest quality, and Thornton's correct use of the orders – Doric on the ground floor and Ionic above – shows surprising sophistication for a provincial architect. Above the doorcases on the side walls are oval frames, while there are no fewer than six carved members in the architrave.

PICTURE

FIRST FLOOR LANDING:

69  *Thomas Ripley* (*c*.1683–1758)
JOSEPH HIGHMORE (1692–1780), signed, 1746
Palladian architect. Born in Yorkshire, rose from carpenter to Comptroller of the King's Works.

NPG 5743

# THE SALOON

A door opposite the head of the secondary stairs leads into the principal upstairs room, occupying the central five bays on the garden side of the house. This 'gallery', as it would probably have been called in the early eighteenth century, would have been used for large gatherings, balls for the county and 'routs' to celebrate important family occasions – births, comings of age and weddings. It would have been sparsely furnished with tables and chairs, introduced as they were required. In the nineteenth century it became a more densely furnished upstairs drawing-room, but the Chesterfields again used the room more formally, with furniture arranged around its edge.

DECORATION

The Saloon is given a strongly architectural feeling by the giant fluted Corinthian pilasters – which enhance the sense of grandeur – and the deeply carved bolection panelling. In the dado this is in the form of large roundels, a rare feature perhaps derived once again from French pattern-books, similar to that found in another Yorkshire house, Kippax Park, demolished in 1953. The skill of

## The Saloon

Thornton's team is again evident in that all the decoration is of carved wood rather than plaster-work. At first sight the half-pilasters meeting in the four corners of the room seem slightly amateur, but the repetition of this motif to emphasise the pair of pilasters flanking the chimney-piece gives the whole scheme unity. The way these two pilasters also project farther into the room, causing the whole entablature to break out over them, is another typically Baroque feature reminiscent of Hawks-moor and Vanbrugh.

The original colour scheme was probably a pale 'silver grey' but the Chesterfields painted the room a strident peacock blue, with the decorative ele-ments of Thornton's carved woodwork picked out in a mixture of gilding and gold paint. The present colour scheme is based on the original. In the early eighteenth century the paler the colour, the more expensive the paint tended to be, so that one can well imagine the very pale blue-grey and plentiful use of gold leaf on the pilasters and frieze being calculated to impress the Bourchiers' less fortunate neighbours.

### CHIMNEY-PIECE

The original chimney-piece was replaced in the nineteenth century, and the present wooden fire-place-surround, marbled in pink and grey, was installed by Lady Chesterfield. The andirons are early eighteenth-century.

### PICTURES

70 *Henry Fox, 1st Baron Holland* (1705–74)
Attributed to JOHN GILES ECCARDT (d.1779), after JEAN-BAPTISTE VAN LOO (1684–1745), *c*.1740
Whig politician; having gambled away his family fortune as a youth, he gained another as Paymaster-General. Father of Charles James Fox. Lent by Lady Teresa Agnew.                                    NPG 2078

71 *Augustus Henry Fitzroy, 3rd Duke of Grafton*
(1735–1811)
POMPEO BATONI (1708–87), Rome, 1762
Prime Minister; a weak successor to Pitt the elder, 1768–9. In the uniform of the West Suffolk Militia. NPG 4899

72 *Thomas Frye* (1710–62)
SELF-PORTRAIT, 1759
Irish portrait-painter and mezzotinter, most notably of fancy heads. Co-founder (1744) and manager (1744–59) of the Bow porcelain factory (the first in England), and inventor of bone china. NPG 5471

73 *Unknown Youth*
JOHN CLOSTERMAN (1660–1711), c.1702–5
NPG 1261

74 *Charles Talbot, 1st Duke of Shrewsbury*
(1660–1718)
After Sir GODFREY KNELLER (1646/9–1723), c.1685
Politician; entertained John Bourchier in Rome.
NPG 1424

75 *David Garrick* (1717–79)
Studio of JOHAN ZOFFANY (1733–1810), c.1763

Actor-manager, particularly at Drury Lane. According to Dr Johnson, his death 'eclipsed the gaiety of nations, and impoverished the public stock of harmless pleasure'. NPG 1167

76 *Abraham Tucker* (1705–74)
ENOCH SEEMAN (1694–1744), signed, 1739
Country gentleman and philosopher; one of the first Utilitarians. NPG 3942

77 *Philip Metcalfe* (1733–1818)
POMPEO BATONI (1708–87), Rome, c.1766–7
Malt distiller, collector and patron of the arts; close friend of Sir Joshua Reynolds. NPG 2001

78 *Catherine Macaulay* (1731–91)
Attributed to ROBERT EDGE PINE (1730–88), c.1774
Historian, known for her *History of England* (1763–83). Friend and admirer of George Washington.
NPG 1357

79 *Henry Stuart, Cardinal York* (1725–1807)
? ITALIAN, c.1750
Son of the 'Old Pretender', younger brother of the 'Young Pretender', and last Stuart claimant to the British throne. See also No. 91. NPG 129

*The Saloon in 1927*

*(81) The Children of John Taylor of Bifrons Park, Kent;*
*by John Closterman, 1696*

OVERDOOR:

80 *Stag Hunting in Galtres Forest*
In the manner of JAN WYCK (1645–1700)
One of the few surviving paintings at Bening-
brough from the Bourchiers' collection.

81 *The Children of John Taylor of Bifrons Park, Kent*
JOHN CLOSTERMAN (1660–1711), 1696
This group is contrived as a play on the Taylor
motto, *Fama candida rosa dulcior* ('fame is sweeter
than a white rose'). The eldest boy (seated at left) is
Brook Taylor (1685–1731), later famous as a
mathematician.                                    NPG 5320

82 *Queen Anne (1665–1714) as Princess of Denmark*
Sir GODFREY KNELLER (1646/9–1723), c.1690
Reigned 1702–14.                                  NPG 1616

83 *Anthony Ashley-Cooper, 3rd Earl of Shaftesbury*
*(1671–1713) and his brother, the Hon. Maurice*
*Ashley-Cooper* (d.1726)
JOHN CLOSTERMAN (1660–1711), c.1700–1?
Moral philosophers, dressed as ancient Greeks.
Shaftesbury (right) and his brother were ardent
Neoplatonists. Their portrait is an expression of
the Neoplatonic commonplace that the beauty of
nature is a visible reflection of the highest beauty,
the mind of God. The Greek inscription on the
temple proclaims that it is dedicated to the Pythian
God, that is Apollo, god of the liberal arts, including
philosophy.                                        NPG 5308

OVERDOOR:

84 *Stag Hunting in Galtres Forest*
In the manner of JAN WYCK (1645–1700)

FURNITURE

A pair of gilt pier-glasses with tripartite glass,
c.1710, from Holme Lacy in the manner of Jean
Pelletier. Chesterfield collection.
A set of gilt Empire chairs and armchairs, the latter

with arm rests supported by griffins, once in the collection of the great French collector Cardinal Fesch and attributed to the French *ébéniste* Georges Jacob. Early nineteenth-century. Duke of Atholl gift.

### CARPET

Irish Doneghal, made for the library of Montalto, Co. Down, c.1910. Lord Clanwilliam gift.

# LADY CHESTERFIELD'S ROOM

This has always been used as a bedroom, originally forming an apartment with the Dressing Room and Closet beyond. Lady Chesterfield kept it painted white rather than stripping the pine as elsewhere in the house. The bolection-moulded panelling has an ornately carved frieze borrowed directly from Daniel Marot's *Nouveau Livre d'Ornaments*, published at The Hague about 1700. The overdoors with their small pedestals, which drop away over the centre of the door, may have been based on a design by Borromini. Thornton's indebtedness to pattern-books is an interesting illustration of the spread of Baroque ornament in England in the early eighteenth century, soon to be replaced by the more correctly classical mouldings of the Palladian school.

### CHIMNEY-PIECE

The contemporary bolection-moulded fire surround is of Derbyshire fossil marble.

### PICTURES

85 *Georgiana Spencer, later Duchess of Devonshire* (1757–1806)
Sir JOSHUA REYNOLDS (1723–92), c.1761
Became a leader of Whig society, famed for her beauty, and notorious for her *ménage à trois* with the 5th Duke and her eventual successor as Duchess, Lady Elizabeth Foster. NPG 1041

OVERDOOR:

86 ?*Frances Bourchier* (1624–76)
ENGLISH, c.1650–5
Wife of Barrington Bourchier (No. 89).

87 *Margaret ('Peg') Woffington* (1714?–60)
ENGLISH, c.1758
Actress; played opposite and became the lover of

*(87) Margaret ('Peg')*
*Woffington; by an unknown*
*English artist, c.1758*

Garrick. Stricken with palsy during her last performance, 1757, and remained bedridden until death.                                            NPG 650

88 *Princess Louisa Maria Theresa Stuart* (1692–1712)

Attributed to NICOLAS DE LARGILLIÈRE (1656–1746)

Only daughter of James II and Mary of Modena.
                                            NPG 1658

OVERDOOR:

89 *?Barrington Bourchier* (1627–80)
ENGLISH, *c*.1650–5
MP and son of Sir John Bourchier, the regicide.

## STATE BED

State bed with original pierced cresting of the tester and elaborately decorated backboard with shell and scrolls, *c*.1680. The crimson damask curtains and coverlet were renewed by Lenygon and Morant in the 1920s. They also made the window curtains with pelmets based on an engraving by Daniel Marot – proof of the knowledge and sensitivity with which this firm approached country-house decoration in the period between the wars. Chesterfield collection.

## FURNITURE

French *bureau Mazarin* in the manner of André Boulle, with brass inlay and tortoiseshell laid on a backing of red paint, late seventeenth-century. Chesterfield collection.

Looking glass with bevelled plate and giltwood frame, *c*.1710. Megaw bequest.

Walnut oval gate-leg table with deep frieze and fold-over top, late seventeenth-century. Megaw bequest.

Two walnut candlestands with octagonal tops, turned stems and tripod feet, late seventeenth-century. Megaw bequest.

Queen Anne daybed with cabriole legs and contemporary *gros point* needlework. Loan from Mr D. Rogers.

Burr walnut tallboy with chased-brass key and handle escutcheons and concave moulding at the base with sunburst motif, early eighteenth-century. Megaw bequest.

Pair of French rococo armchairs with bowed seat rails, cabriole legs and cross-shaped stretchers. *Gros*

*point* needlework, mid-eighteenth-century. Ullstein loan.

French travelling toilet box in bird's-eye maple, made for Lady Chesterfield. It is inscribed 'Tonnel, Paris'.

Eighteenth-century-style French stool with needlework cover. Ullstein loan.

## CERAMICS

ON TALLBOY:
Chinese *famille rose* vase, Yongzheng, *c*.1730. Bushell bequest.

ON CHIMNEY-PIECE:

Three Chinese *famille rose* plates, late eighteenth-century. Fox bequest.

## CARPET

A Persian Kerman carpet, with multiple borders and medallions and spandrels on a pale blue field, late nineteenth- or early twentieth-century.

# LADY CHESTERFIELD'S DRESSING ROOM

This room is the same shape as the two corner dressing-rooms on the ground floor and is equally elaborately decorated with a boldly carved frieze, bolection panelling in very high relief and an angled chimney-piece with stepped tiers above it. The decoration – white, with the mouldings of the panelling and architraves picked out in blue – was done with a view to having blue-and-white china on the mantelpiece and was carried out with the advice of John Fowler, just before his death in 1977.

## CHIMNEY-PIECE

An early eighteenth-century marble bolection-moulded surround with later eighteenth-century Carron cast-iron hob grate.

## PICTURES

90 *Prince Charles Edward Stuart* (1720–88)
Studio of ANTONIO DAVID (1684?–1750), *c*.1729
'Bonnie Prince Charlie', 'the Young Pretender'; grandson of James II, and eldest son of the 'Old Pretender'. Led the abortive Rising of 1745.
                                            NPG 434

91 *Henry Stuart, Cardinal York* (1725–1807)
Studio of ANTONIO DAVID (1684?–1750), *c*.1729
Son of the 'Old Pretender'. Younger brother of
No. 90 above.                                    NPG 435

92 *Joseph Gibbs* (1699–1788)
THOMAS GAINSBOROUGH (1727–88), *c*.1755
Organist of St Mary, Ipswich, and composer of
violin sonatas; friend of the artist.            NPG 2179

93 *Admiral Edward ('Grog') Vernon* (1684–1757)
THOMAS GAINSBOROUGH (1727–88), *c*.1753
Captured Porto Bello (1739); introduced the diluted
naval rum ration known as 'grog' (one part rum to
four parts water), apparently from his characteristic
garb of a grogram cloak.                         NPG 881

94 *Admiral Edward Boscawen* (1711–61)
Sir JOSHUA REYNOLDS (1723–92), *c*.1755
Victor of Louisbourg (1758) and Lagos Bay (1759),
known as 'Dreadnought'. Builder of Hatchlands,
Surrey (NT).                                     NPG 5302

### FURNITURE

Three Dutch marquetry side chairs, early eighteenth-century.
A rococo mahogany commode with shaped serpentine front, cabriole legs and elaborate ormolu
mounts, probably north German, *c*.1745.

### CERAMICS

Chinese large blue-and-white bowl, Kangxi, early
eighteenth-century. Ashmolean loan.

ON CHIMNEY-PIECE:

Chinese blue-and-white porcelain, mostly Kangxi,
early eighteenth-century, and Ming, mid-seven-
teenth-century. Ashmolean loan and Bushell bequest. (Room stewards have further details.)

### CARPET

A modern Turkey rug in combined medallion and
other Ushak designs.

## LADY CHESTERFIELD'S BATHROOM

The Closet adjoining the Dressing Room was fitted
up as a bathroom by Lady Chesterfield in the 1920s,
with stippled apricot-coloured decoration, perhaps
by Lenygon & Morant, slate tiles and a sunk bath,
something of an innovation at this period. How-

*The carved marble bowl in Lady Chesterfield's Bathroom
may once have belonged to the niche in the vestibule outside*

ever, the round-headed niche with a brass water
spout and carved marble bowl beneath it appears to
be original and a rare example therefore of an early
eighteenth-century buffet fountain. The closet to a
bedchamber would have been a curious place to
find such a feature and it may originally have come
from the vestibule outside, where a curious stove-
like projection set across one corner has a similar,
now meaningless, niche.

## THE READING ROOM

This room, in the north-west corner of the house,
may originally have been an upstairs dining parlour,
which would explain the purpose of the *buffet* for
washing hands in the lobby outside. The panelling
and cornice are plain compared with those elsewhere in the house, although the deep relief of the
mouldings creates an effect of light and shade that is
rare in provincial joinery. The room has now been
decorated and furnished (with the aid of a generous
grant from the Merchant Staplers Company of
Bradford) as somewhere where visitors may rest,
and read or write, before ascending to the National
Portrait Gallery exhibition on the second floor.

## CHIMNEY-PIECE

The contemporary fire surround is of grey Derbyshire marble with fossils clearly embedded in it. The iron hob grate by the Carron Company is later eighteenth-century.

## PICTURES

95 *Edwyn, 10th Earl of Chesterfield* (1854–1933)
FRANCISQUE-EDOUARD BERTIER (fl.1879–90), signed, 1890
Moved to Beningbrough with his wife (No.99) in 1917.

96 *Philip, 4th Earl of Chesterfield* (1694–1773)
WILLIAM HOARE OF BATH (c.1707–99)
See No. 59 for biography.

97 *Elizabeth Davies* (née *Cattle*)
ORAZIO MANARA (1804–after 1872), signed, 1847
Wife of Robert Davies, FSA, of York.

99 *Enid, Countess of Chesterfield* (1878–1957)
ELLIS ROBERTS (1860–1930), signed, 1900
Wife of the 10th Earl (No.95), painted in the year of her marriage. Lived at Beningbrough until her death in 1957.

## SCULPTURE

98 *Unknown woman*
Sir JOHN STEELL (1804–91), signed, 1851
Marble bust

# THE UPPER CORRIDOR

The lobby between the Bathroom and the Reading Room has carved decoration as rich and individual as anywhere in the house. Two pairs of pierced console brackets with acanthus embellishment are particularly striking. Two open arches, with a shallow saucer dome in the bay between them, frame the vista from one end of the house to the other. As on the ground floor the sense of perspective along the vista is again exaggerated, this time by a series of stepped pilasters.

## SCULPTURE

Bronze bust of the Roman Emperor Vespasian.

## CERAMICS

Large Chinese blue-and-white beaker vase, Kangxi, early eighteenth-century.

# THE GREAT STAIRCASE

On the upper landing of the Great Staircase the marquetry panel with the initials 'REB' and the Bourchier reef-knot framed in the plasterwork is one of the few relics of the sixteenth-century house at Beningbrough built by Sir Ralph Bourchier. This may have inspired the later marquetry panels inlaid with the Bourchier arms and the date 1716, which can be seen on the two half-landings of the staircase below.

## PICTURE

100 *Captain James Cornewall* (1699–1744)
ENGLISH, c.1730–40
Killed in action off Toulon.                NPG 5323

# THE ATTIC FLOOR

Returning through the Saloon, visitors ascend to the attic floor. This is now part of the National Portrait Gallery's exhibition, but the rooms were probably intended originally as lesser family bedrooms rather than as servants' garrets. Several of the rooms have oak panelling from the Elizabethan manor house, which was reused by John Bourchier in his new mansion. These would no doubt have provided effective insulation from the cold and draughts of a Yorkshire winter.

## PICTURES AND SCULPTURE
### *The Portrait and the Country House*

The display on the top floor has been arranged by the National Portrait Gallery to illustrate the development of portraiture between 1688 and 1760 in terms of social and architectural history.

### ROOM 1
### *The Portrait*

This room, to the left at the head of the stairs, is devoted to the different media employed by portraitists – paintings, sculpture, pastels, drawings and miniatures – and the prices patrons would be expected to pay for portraits of varying sizes and

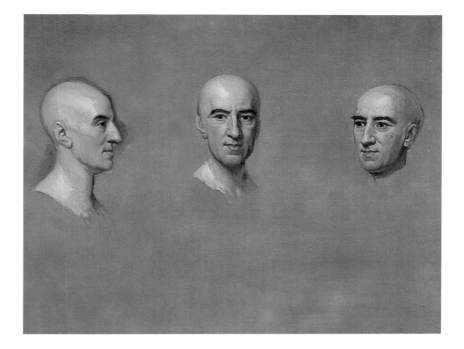

*(101) Daniel Finch,
2nd Earl of Nottingham
and 7th Earl of
Winchilsea; by
Sir Godfrey Kneller,
c.1720?*

including particular accessories, such as a dog or a view of a house. It also demonstrates the shift from formal to informal portraiture characteristic of the age of Rococo. Both types of portrait, however, continued to flourish side by side, and were often employed by the same artist. From time-to-time changes will be made in the display to minimise the risk of light-sensitive works on paper suffering from fading or deterioration.

101 *Daniel Finch, 2nd Earl of Nottingham and 7th Earl of Winchilsea* (1647–1730)
Sir GODFREY KNELLER (1646/9–1723), c.1720?
A moderate Tory, Nottingham was alienated by James II's extremism; his faithfulness to the Revolution Settlement saved many Tories from becoming Jacobites. NPG 3910

102 *?John Gay* (1685–1732)
Attributed to Sir GODFREY KNELLER (1646/9–1723)
Poet and dramatist; author of *The Beggar's Opera*. NPG 622

103 *Laurence Sterne* (1713–68)
ENGLISH, c.1760?
Novelist and prebendary of York; author of *Tristram Shandy* and *A Sentimental Journey*. NPG 2022

104 *Alexander Pope* (1688–1744)
WILLIAM HOARE OF BATH (c.1707–99), 1784, based on a pastel of 1739
Pastel
The foremost poet of the Augustan age (see also No. 49). NPG 299

105 *Elizabeth Carter* (1717–1806)
Sir THOMAS LAWRENCE (1769–1830), 1788–9
Pastel
Learned in scripture and the classics, she translated Epictetus and contributed to the *Gentleman's Magazine*. NPG 28

106 *Edward Gibson* (1657–1701)
SELF-PORTRAIT, signed, 1690
Chalk
An obscure, but evidently talented artist; this is one of his few surviving works. NPG 1880

107 *Prince James Francis Edward Stuart* (1688–1766)
FRANCESCO PONZONE (fl.1741), Rome, c.1741
Pen and black ink
'The Old Pretender'; only son of James II, he headed the Jacobite invasion of 1715. NPG 4535

108 *John Vanderbank* (1694?–1739)
SELF-PORTRAIT, signed, 1738
Pen and brown ink
Painter of portraits and of illustrations to *Don*

*Quixote*. His sitters included Queen Caroline and Sir Isaac Newton. NPG 3647

109 *James Wolfe* (1727–59)
Modern bronze cast of a bust by JOSEPH WILTON (1722–1803), c.1759
General; killed in the capture of Quebec, a victory which ended French rule in Canada. NPG 2225

110 *James Wolfe* (1727–59)
The Hon. HAROLD DILLON (1844–1932) after a drawing attributed to Sir HERVEY SMITH (1734–1811), c.1759
A copy of one of the few portraits of Wolfe from the life. NPG 713a

111 *John Michael Rysbrack* (1693–1770)
JOHN VANDERBANK (1694?–1739), c.1728
Sculptor; born and died in Antwerp but in England by 1720, and soon the acknowledged head of his profession, with a large output of busts, monuments, chimney-pieces and decorative sculpture. NPG 1802

112 *James McArdell* (1729?–65)
Sir JOSHUA REYNOLDS (1723–92), c.1756–60
One of the greatest of eighteenth-century mezzo-tinters, he engraved many plates after portraits by Reynolds. He is shown at work on his plate from Van Dyck's *Time clipping the Wings of Love*. NPG 3123

113 *William, Duke of Cumberland* (1721–65)
CHARLES JERVAS (c.1675–1739), c.1728
Third son of George II, wearing the robes and collar of a Knight of the Bath; he later defeated Prince Charles, 'The Young Pretender', at Culloden in 1746. NPG 802

114 *The Talman Family*
GIUSEPPE GRISONI (1699–1769), c.1718–19
From left: William Talman (1650–1719), architect; John Talman (1677–1726), antiquary; Frances Cockayne (d.1733); and Hannah Talman. The mythological figures presumably represent the gods blessing the marriage of John Talman to Frances Cockayne in 1718. NPG 5781

## ROOM 2

### Architecture

The left side of the corridor is concerned with the principal phases in the development of architecture in the late seventeenth century and the eighteenth century – Baroque, Palladian and Neo-classical – with a portrait of John Carr of York, who was associated with Robert Adam in the building of Harewood House, completing the sequence at the end. On the right are shown the decorators, from Verrio to Angelica Kauffmann, and the authors of the treatises and manuals on architecture which were responsible for the proliferation of the 'Georgian' style throughout Britain.

115 *Sir Thomas Robinson, Bt* (c.1702–77)
FRANS VAN DER MIJN (1719–83), 1750
An amateur architect and admirer of Palladian principles, he rebuilt his Yorkshire house, Rokeby. For his father-in-law, the 3rd Earl of Carlisle, he designed the west wing of Castle Howard, also in Yorkshire. NPG 5275

116 *Charles Howard, 3rd Earl of Carlisle* (1669–1738)
Sir GODFREY KNELLER (1646/9–1723), signed in monogram, c.1712
A firm supporter of William and Mary and a patron of Vanbrugh to whom he gave the commission for Castle Howard; he helped negotiate the Treaty of Union with Scotland, 1707. The Kit-cat portrait. NPG 3197

117 *Sir John Vanbrugh* (1664–1726)
Attributed to THOMAS MURRAY, c.1718
Architect and playwright, he built Castle Howard and designed Blenheim Palace for the 1st Duke of Marlborough. He wears a herald's badge. NPG 1568

118 *Richard Boyle, 3rd Earl of Burlington* (1694–1753)
After Sir GODFREY KNELLER (1646/9–1723)
Patron of the arts, and architect; chief advocate of the Palladian style. Seen here as a child with his sister, Lady Jane Boyle. NPG 2495

119 *Isaac Ware* (c.1707?–66)
After LOUIS FRANÇOIS ROUBILIAC (c.1705–62)
Plaster cast
Architect and writer on architecture; he designed a London house, demolished in 1937, for the 4th Earl of Chesterfield (No. 59, Blue Bedroom). NPG

120 *John Carr* (1723–1807)
Sir WILLIAM BEECHEY (1753–1839), c.1791
'Carr of York', architect of many comfortable and distinguished houses, public buildings and bridges in Yorkshire and the north of England. In the background is the church of Horbury, Yorkshire, erected at Carr's own expense, 1791–3. NPG 4062

*(123) Self-portrait;*
*by Angelica*
*Kauffmann, c.1778?*

121  *Antonio Verrio* (1639?–1707)
SELF-PORTRAIT, *c.*1705
Decorative painter; born in Italy, came to England and worked at Windsor Castle and at Burghley House. The inscription – meaning 'Here is Antonio, Oh poor Verrio' – probably refers to the failure of his eyesight late in life.                    NPG 2890

122  *Grinling Gibbons* (1648–1720)
After Sir GODFREY KNELLER (1646/9–1723)
Virtuoso wood carver and sculptor.        NPG 2925

123  *Angelica Kauffmann* (1741–1807)
SELF-PORTRAIT, *c.*1778?
Swiss decorative painter; in London by 1765, she became friendly with Reynolds and was elected a Royal Academician.                          NPG 430

124  *James Gibbs* (1682–1754)
JOHN MICHAEL WILLIAMS (fl.1743–66), signed, *c.*1752?
Architect of Cannons, St Martin-in-the-Fields and the Radcliffe Library, Oxford; his influential *Book of Architecture* was published in 1728. He points to a plan of the Radcliffe Library.            NPG 504

125 *Francis Price* (1704?–53)
GEORGE BEARE (fl.1743–9), signed, 1747
Author of *The British Carpenter*, 1733, and Surveyor of Salisbury Cathedral; he holds a drawing for one of the transept roof-trusses.                    NPG 1960

### ROOM 3
### 'Who was Who'

This is the largest gallery on the top floor and once contained several small servants' bedrooms. It commands a fine view north to the Hambleton Hills. The different types of portrait shown in this room demonstrate the niceties of social status in the eighteenth century.

126 *Sir Godfrey Kneller* (1646/9–1723)
SELF-PORTRAIT, *c*.1709–11
Kneller captured the fashionable portrait market on the death of Lely in 1680, and painted every king and queen from Charles II to George II, the last as Prince of Wales. In the background is Kneller Hall, the house he built at Whitton, Middlesex.

NPG 3214

127 *Louis François Roubiliac* (*c*.1705–62)
ADRIAEN CARPENTIERS (fl.1739–78), signed, 1762
The greatest of English rococo portrait sculptors, Roubiliac came to London from Paris about 1730. He is at work on the model for the marble statue of Shakespeare made for the temple in David Garrick's garden at Hampton. The marble is now in the British Library and the model in the Victoria and Albert Museum.                    NPG 303

128 *Sir William Chambers* (1723–96)
Sir JOSHUA REYNOLDS (1723–92), *c*.1755
Architect of Somerset House, The Strand; a founder member of the Royal Academy of Arts and the principal rival of Robert Adam.         NPG 27

129 *Francis Ayscough* (1700–63) *with his pupils, the Prince of Wales (later George III) and the Duke of York*
RICHARD WILSON (1713–82), *c*.1749
The two eldest sons of Frederick, Prince of Wales, and Princess Augusta (see Nos 7 and 4). The canvas was cut *c*.1917, dividing the two boys from their tutor, and reunited in 1976; the top right portion with the columns is a modern reconstruction.

NPG 1165

130 *Robert Wood* (1716–71)
ALLAN RAMSAY (1713–84), signed, Rome, 1755
Classical archaeologist, MP and author of *The Ruins of Palmyra* and *The Ruins of Baalbec*.       NPG 4868

131 *Matthew Prior* (1664–1721)
After JONATHAN RICHARDSON (*c*.1665–1745), *c*.1718
Diplomat; he negotiated much of the Peace of Utrecht; also a poet, collector and friend of Edward Harley, 2nd Earl of Oxford (No. 139).       NPG 562

132 *Christopher Anstey* (1724–1805) *and his daughter, Mary*
WILLIAM HOARE OF BATH (*c*.1707–99), *c*.1775
Country gentleman and author; best known for his witty *New Bath Guide*, a rhymed satire of life in the spa; his daughter holds a doll with hair dressed in the outrageous style of the mid-1770s, the subject of another of Anstey's comic poems.       NPG 3084

133 *Samuel Richardson* (1698–1761)
JOSEPH HIGHMORE (1692–1780), *c*.1747
Novelist and printer; his three novels, *Pamela, Clarissa Harlowe* and *Sir Charles Grandison*, enjoyed enormous popularity.       NPG 161

134 *John Perceval, 2nd Earl of Egmont* (1711–70)
THOMAS HUDSON (1701–79), *c*.1758
Political supporter of Frederick, Prince of Wales, and a clever pamphleteer.       NPG 2481

135 *John Christopher Pepusch* (1667–1752)
THOMAS HUDSON (1701–79), *c*.1735
Composer; born in Berlin; Master of the Music to the Duke of Chandos at Cannons, 1712, and later wrote for the opera in Lincoln's Inn Fields. He wears the gown of an Oxford Doctor of Music.

NPG 2063

136 *Joseph Kelway* (d.1782?)
JOHN RUSSELL (1745–1806), signed, 1776, after ANDREA SOLDI (*c*.1703–71)
Pastel
Organist of St Martin-in-the-Fields; a virtuoso keyboard player, he taught Queen Charlotte and Mrs Delany (No. 146).       NPG 4213

### ROOM 4
### *Collectors*

This room, at the end of the corridor on the right, is hung with portraits of some of the great collectors of the age, together with examples of the works of art they amassed. Especially revealing is the contrast between the tastes of Sir Robert Walpole and his son

*(132) Christopher Anstey and his daughter, Mary; by William Hoare of Bath, c.1775*

*(146) Mrs Mary Delany;*
*by John Opie, c.1782*

Horace. The former housed his collection of fine Old Masters in a Palladian country home in Norfolk. The latter collected curiosities and ancient furniture to embellish a Gothick villa, Strawberry Hill, in the environs of London, a creation which was his life work and to which he was always ready to admit visitors.

137 *Jonathan Richardson (1665–1745)*
SELF-PORTRAIT, 1729
Portrait-painter, collector of Old Master drawings and author of several influential works on painting and taste. NPG 706

138 *William Cavendish, 2nd Duke of Devonshire (1673–1729)*
Sir GODFREY KNELLER (1646/9–1723), signed in monogram, c.1710–16
Acquired many of the drawings at Chatsworth, making it one of the finest collections of its day. The Kit-cat portrait, showing the Duke with the white staff of office of the Lord Steward of the Household.
NPG 3202

139 *Edward Harley, 2nd Earl of Oxford* (1689–1741)
GEORGE VERTUE (1683–1756), 1746, after
MICHAEL DAHL (1656/9–1743)
Engraving
Collector and patron, he inherited and added to his father's famous Harleian library; their manuscripts formed the nucleus of the British Museum collections; he holds a medal of Queen Anne. Harley owned Wimpole Hall, Cambridgeshire (NT). NPG

140 *George Vertue* (1683–1756)
M. GAUCI (fl.1810–46), 1821, after GEORGE VERTUE, 1741
Lithograph
Engraver and antiquary; his notebooks provide the most important record of British art before 1750. He holds a miniature of his patron, the 2nd Earl of Oxford. NPG

141 *Richard Mead* (1673–1753)
JONATHAN RICHARDSON (1665–1745), c.1738
The leading physician of his day and a great collector, especially of classical antiquities. NPG 4157

142 *Horace Walpole, 4th Earl of Orford* (1717–97)
T. EVANS after Sir THOMAS LAWRENCE (1769–1830), 1796
Stipple engraving
The varied collection he assembled at Strawberry Hill had a strong interest in British history. His witty and voluminous correspondence presents an unrivalled picture of English society life for nearly half a century. NPG

ROOM 5

*Life beyond the house*

In this room the history of the landscape garden is traced. Engravings from *Costumes of Yorkshire Illustrated*, 1814, show the dress of farmers and labourers, and photographs of Hogarth's *Election* series display something of the seamier side of contemporary life.

143 *Richard Temple, 1st Viscount Cobham* (1675–1749)
After JEAN-BAPTISTE VAN LOO (1684–1745), c.1740
Served with distinction under Marlborough and in Spain; dismissed by Sir Robert Walpole, he devoted his energies to the redevelopment of the house and garden at Stowe in Buckinghamshire. NPG 286

144 *Lancelot ('Capability') Brown* (1716–83)
NATHANIEL DANCE (1735–1811), c.1770
'Naturalised' the park at Stowe; his influence as a landscape gardener is still to be seen in the parks of many country houses. NPG 1490

145 *William Kent* (1685?–1748)
BARTHOLOMEW DANDRIDGE (1691–c.1755), signed, c.1736?
Architect of the Horse-Guards, the Treasury and the Royal Mews, and of country houses, where he had an important influence on landscape gardening. NPG 1557

146 *Mrs Mary Delany* (1700–88)
JOHN OPIE (1761–1807), c.1782
Celebrated for her 'flower mosaics' made from intricately cut paper; her correspondence gives a lively picture of eighteenth-century society. Painted for the Countess of Bute; the frame designed by Horace Walpole. NPG 1030

147 *Sir Charles Hanbury Williams* (1708–59)
Attributed to JOHN GILES ECCARDT (d.1779), c.1746
Satirical writer, MP and diplomat. NPG 383

148 *Jonas Hanway* (1712–86)
JAMES NORTHCOTE (1746–1831), c.1785
Traveller and philanthropist; a founder of the Marine Society and a pioneer of the umbrella. NPG 4301

149 *John ('Jack') Sheppard* (1700–24)
GEORGE WHITE (1684?–1732) after Sir JAMES THORNHILL (1675–1734), c.1724
Mezzotint
Robber and highwayman; preyed mainly on London and the suburbs. NPG

CERAMICS

Four Chinese blue-and-white hexagonal pierced jars with lids.
Large Chinese Imperial bottle decorated with peaches, Qianlong, later eighteenth-century. Ashmolean loan.

# THE LAUNDRY

Visitors descend to the ground floor via a servants' stair, ingeniously fitted into a tiny space next to the Great Staircase, and leave the house through the front door. The arch to the left under the Bell Tower leads to the laundry yard, which, before the restoration in the late 1970s, was overgrown and surrounded by derelict buildings. The yard has now

*The Laundry*

been recobbled and the coach-house and Laundry
restored.

The latter contains its original nineteenth-
century arrangement of 'wet' and 'dry' rooms. The
smaller wet room, to the right, has two boilers
heated by a fire below. The larger one, into which
water was pumped, was probably used for boiling
clothes, while the smaller one provided water for
general washing. The wooden sinks originally had
copper taps. The wooden implement, resembling a
four- or six-legged stool with a handle and crossbar
is a Dolly, which was twisted backwards and
forwards in a wooden or zinc dolly tub to force
soapy water through dirty clothes. The Poss Stick,
made from a solid piece of wood and widening to a
cylinder with four cuts, beat the dirt out of clothes.
It was superseded by the copper bell-shaped posser,
which cleaned by suction when moved up and

down in the wash tub. The fluted zinc washing
boards were used for scrubbing very dirty clothes.

In the dry room, to the left, is an iron-framed
mangle with two rollers. It could be used for either
wringing wet clothes or pressing dry ones. In the
centre of the room the box mangle, containing
stones, pressed large damp sheets or tableclothes
with wooden rollers fitted under the box. The room
also includes a selection of box, flat and polishing
irons, and a goffering machine for giving a neat
finish to frills. To the left of the boiler are two more
hand-operated washing machines dating from the
early twentieth century.

# CHAPTER EIGHT

# THE GROUNDS AND GARDEN

Beningbrough lies in the fertile flood plain of the River Ouse, in the midst of the Vale of York. The origins of the estate are obscure, but undoubtedly ancient, dating back at least to the possession of the estate by the monks of St Leonard's Hospital, York, in the twelfth century. The medieval park contained areas used for arable farming and garden produce, an agricultural enclave in the heart of the Forest of Galtres. In the seventeenth century canals were dug across part of this flat landscape, but otherwise it probably changed little until the building of the present house, when the landscape was formalised by the planting of grand avenues centering on the house. The late eighteenth and early nineteenth centuries saw the removal of the formal elements of the landscape, which was altered to the English style of 'Capability' Brown and Humphry Repton.

In Victorian times, Lord and Lady Downe created intimate flower gardens around the house; the garden enjoyed another period of glory under Lord and Lady Chesterfield from 1917 until the death of Lady Chesterfield in 1957. However, the dearth of estate records has meant that only a sketchy record of garden and grounds survives, tantalisingly incomplete and open to conjecture.

Some authors have suggested that a Roman military road runs through the estate and that this contains the remains of a Roman villa but there remains no proof. In the Domesday book Beningbrough land is given as 180 acres in size, much smaller than the estate referred to in later monastic records. The improvement in written records from the 1270s onwards gives us a clearer picture of the extent and character of the estate, helped particularly by a manorial survey of Beningbrough made in 1287. The estate lay within a royal forest, the Forest of Galtres, which was not owned by the Crown, but over which the King had hunting and other rights.

In 1284 the brethren of St Leonard's were granted permission to enclose a further 100 acres of their own land and 56½ acres of adjoining woodland to create the 'new park of Beningburg', an area which appears on old maps as the Old Deer Park north-east of the house, beyond the present park. This brought the area of land farmed by the brethren to some 540 acres, of which 366 were arable land and pasture, a small part being meadow mown for hay, and an area near the Grange – the building from which the estate was run – being used for orchards and kitchen gardens. The site of the Grange is not known: it might have been south-east of the present house where the Elizabethan house of Sir Ralph Bourchier was built or possibly in the area that appears as a discontinuity in the ridges and furrows of the medieval farming system which show up in aerial photographs.

The estate had its own windmill, and flour and other produce would have been sent down river to St Leonard's Landing in York. There were also rights to graze livestock in the surrounding forest, including 'pannage' which allowed pigs to be fed on fallen acorns from September to November each year. Rights of 'husbot and haybot' allowed a certain amount of wood to be taken from the forest for building hedges and houses.

The ancient origins of the estate and the fact that it has never been entirely cleared of trees and woodland have ensured a rich diversity of flora and fauna. Insects associated with ancient woodland are well represented, including a spider-hunting wasp (*Dipogon subintermedius*), one of the species of spectacular Red Cardinal beetles and the Purple Hairstreak butterfly.

Sadly, nothing is recorded of the grounds or garden that must have surrounded the Elizabethan house Sir Ralph Bourchier built at Beningbrough. In 1633 the inclusion of a substantial part of the

*The park to the south of the house still reflects the informal planting of the late eighteenth and early nineteenth centuries*

Beningbrough estate within the royal deer park planned by Sir Thomas Wentworth sent Sir Ralph's grandson, the eccentric Sir John Bourchier, into a fury. His protests brought fines and imprisonment, and turned him permanently against the Crown; in 1649 Sir John was one of the signatories of the King's death warrant.

Had Sir John not died just before the Restoration in 1660, the family might have lost the Beningbrough estate; however, his son Barrington was an ardent royalist, giving active support to the Restoration and so the estate remained intact. The various stew ponds which appear in the 1852 Ordnance Survey map may well have been made at about this time, or even earlier, and could have been decorative as well as useful. The Carp Pond, aligned on an axis due north of the Elizabethan house, could once have been an ornamental canal. This has since been filled in but the Tench Pond survives, at right angles to the axis of the Carp Pond. The three Pike Ponds once had a complex system of interconnecting sluices, perhaps needed to keep a food source and young and mature pikes separate.

When the present house was completed in 1716,

the formal style of landscape design still reigned supreme and the more natural style of Lancelot 'Capability' Brown was yet to come. Although little is recorded of the Beningbrough landscape, early maps show the grand avenues which were typical of the period: a single avenue of Common Lime (*Tilia × europaea*) marched away from the house to the north; the walk along the south front of the house was extended to the west by another avenue, combining with a further three to the south-west (towards the Nun Monkton ferry), south and south-east to create a *patte d'oie*, or goose-foot, of *allées*, a feature often found in landscapes of the time, most notably at Hampton Court. The route from the ferry would have been an important access and boats would still have been a convenient means of transport at this period, particularly for visitors coming from York.

We know from later accounts that some of these avenues were of oak, but there are also nineteenth-century accounts which mention ancient elms east of the house and suggest they were 'remains of avenues'; it is possible that these were the last vestiges of planting relating to the Elizabethan house, perhaps introduced when the passion for formal gardening swept the country in the late seventeenth century.

No accounts of the garden made for the new house have come to light, although an intriguing sketch of about 1720 made by Samuel Buck survives showing a parterre design which may or may not have existed south of the house. (Owners would often choose not to implement such plans, perhaps through lack of funds, but more probably because of the rapid changes in taste in garden design at the time.)

Buck's sketch shows a design of four large compartments divided by a broad path running southwards from the house and an east–west cross path terminated by a splendid gate. The compartments near the house would have been *parterres de broderie*, elaborately scrolled Baroque designs of box edging possibly infilled with coloured gravels. The two further compartments are shown as beds of simpler shapes which would also probably have been box-edged. Each compartment is surrounded by a narrow border or *plate bande*, probably edged

with box, planted with flowers and punctuated with topiary cones of evergreens. At the far end of the garden is 'a Fine Channel' or canal running east–west, which seems to have borders and a path on either side. Railings are shown separating the garden from the park. The extent of the garden appears to be considerable, stretching well beyond the position of the present ha-ha.

The plan drawn by Buck would have been thought rather old-fashioned when it was proposed and it does not seem to relate well to, and might therefore have predated, the pattern of radiating avenues which lay beyond; no access is shown to the south avenue across the canal or through a gate in the railings. It is interesting to see the east pavilion in the sketch, indicating that this had been built by

*Samuel Buck's sketch of about 1720 shows formal parterres south of the house*

then, although Buck has shown a different finial to the one appearing in Bouttats and Chapman's painting of 1751. This same painting also shows splendid stables and outbuildings symmetrically enclosing the north forecourt of the house. It is not certain whether these were ever built; if they were, it is hard to conceive why any owner should want to remove such fine buildings. However, they might have been thought to interfere with oblique views of the house once the drives and north park had been remodelled in the English landscape style.

When the estate passed to the last of the Beningbrough Bourchiers, Margaret, and her husband Giles Earle, in the early 1760s, avenues and formal gardens were out of fashion. It is likely that such young occupants, with every expectancy of seeing new planting reaching maturity, would have wanted to make changes, but it seems that the Earles were cautious in their approach, leaving the avenues perhaps as a nurse for new planting or to grow sufficiently to produce saleable timber. The avenues still appear in Jeffrey's *Map of England* (1767–70).

A French visitor to Beningbrough in June 1768 described the gardens:

Walked in the gardens which are very pretty with water and the river below. Fine bowling green, beautiful menagerie with pheasants, fine lawn and bosquets of foreign trees, heated glasshouses for pineapples. Magnificent outbuildings, beautiful stables, beautiful allée of oaks in a field in front of the house – with irregular clumps of trees but making a charming effect to either side of the allée. Beautiful English greenery which no other country can match.

It is perhaps significant that there is no mention of formal gardens or flowers and the 'irregular clumps' may have been recent planting in the informal English landscape style, designed to be seen to full effect once the avenues were taken away. The reference to water in the garden is tantalising: was this the canal shown by Buck or just the pond east of the house which appears in the first Ordnance Survey map of 1852? And what of the magnificent outbuildings and beautiful stables? These were probably the ones shown by Bouttats and Chapman, not the present stable block, which dates from the late eighteenth century and may have been

built by Peter Atkinson, a pupil of John Carr of York.

In December 1778, Giles Earle, who was often short of money, offered for sale a 'large quantity of oak timber (for ship building) with some ash, elm and sycamore trees, growing on or near the Ouse in Beningbrough, Newton, Overton and Shipton'.

The Newton entrance lodge is an almost exact copy of one built at Thirkleby Hall near Thirsk in the 1790s for Sir Thomas Frankland and probably designed by James Wyatt. It is likely that much of the landscaping of the entrance drive and the north park dates from this period. Successful landscaping on such a flat site is difficult, but the apparent lack of distinction of the design suggests it was made by the Earles themselves or their land agent rather than a professional landscaper. The rather straight drive from Newton gate would have offered few opportunities for the varied and carefully composed views of the house, which were a feature of the best designed drives of Brown or Repton, and seems to have aimed in a rather unsatisfactory way at the west pavilion rather than the house itself. These shortcomings may have led to the reinstatement of the north avenue early this century, keeping the house hidden until its dramatic appearance framed at the end of an avenue of limes.

Earle is portrayed unflatteringly in a novel about Beningbrough written by J. L. Armstrong in 1836; referring to the estate as it was in the late seventeenth century, Armstrong writes of tall elms east of the hall and of a beech avenue beside the Ouse which may have been one of those shown in Jeffrey's map or perhaps the wooded walk which ran round the perimeter of the estate. The southern section of this walk, known as The Belt, is unusual in that then, as now, it completely blocked views to the river and the countryside beyond. Most landscape designers would have been eager to open at least a few glimpses through this belt to the river and the 'borrowed landscape' beyond, creating distant views from the house.

In a letter written to his attorney at law, Joseph Munby, in 1806, Giles Earle described a prank perpetrated with the help of his Head Gardener, Leonard Urquhart, in which he stole a China Orange tree from a Mr Hotham in York and

*The pear avenue in the Kitchen Garden*

brought it by boat to Beningbrough. The shock was too much for the orange which promptly dropped its flowers and fruit, to Earle's dismay. By 1809 Urquhart had left his employment as a citrus rustler to set up his own nursery in York.

With the death of Margaret Earle in 1827, Beningbrough passed to her distant cousin, the Rev. William Henry Dawnay, later 6th Viscount Downe. Dawnay appears to have been particularly active in instigating new planting in the following years and many existing trees seem to date from this period.

An unsigned and undated report on the grounds accompanied by 'before and after' sketches has been shown to be by William Sawrey Gilpin, the nephew and pupil of the Rev. William Gilpin, the pioneer of the Picturesque landscape. Most of Gilpin's recommendations, such as opening views to the river and Nun Monkton through the belt and creating a terrace wall south of the house, seem to have been ignored; however, there are marked similarities between the planting he favoured and that which survives, notably some of the cedars, thorns and the positions of clumps.

Thomas Foster (1798–1866) worked as Head Gardener for Dawnay from 1824, apparently coming to Beningbrough in 1827 when Dawnay inherited. He evidently brought the gardens to a high standard of horticultural excellence, winning frequent prizes at the York Horticultural Society show, particularly for fruit, vegetables and dahlias. His most outstanding success was the raising in about 1835 of two new varieties of glasshouse grape from a cross between 'Black Morocco' and 'White

Sweetwater'. 'Lady Downe's Seedling', a sweet and richly flavoured white, is often rated the finest late-keeping glasshouse grape, ripening in August but keeping on the vine in good condition until the following March. 'Foster's Seedling' is also white, sweet and well-flavoured and perhaps the best early grape; it was traditionally produced in royal glass-houses for Queen Mary, to be presented to her each year on her birthday, 26 May. Both varieties now grow in the vinery in the walled garden.

The estate map of 1841, probably a few years after Gilpin's visit, shows tree-planting predomin-antly in the informal landscape style, although with several straight lines of trees (perhaps not avenues, but the remains of old hedgerows). The main avenues of Jeffrey's 1767–70 map have gone, with the possible exception of the four parallel rows running westwards towards the river from the west pleasure ground. This area with its circuit path, now the Adventure Playground, already appears planted

*The east formal garden*

with trees. Another four parallel rows are shown running from this pleasure ground towards Nun Monkton but stopping before the edge of the inner (sheep) park then known as Well Garth. The various stew ponds for pike, carp and tench are the only water features indicated. The house and kitchen garden are shown surrounded by typical Victorian pleasure grounds (although these might date from the time of the Earles). The walled garden appears with an extension or 'slip' to the south. The area south and east of this and bounded by the ha-ha is intersected by paths and planted with trees.

In 1848, two years after the estate had passed to Lord Downe's son Payan Dawnay, Beningbrough was surveyed for the first Ordnance Survey map which appeared in 1852. The new map shows several changes from the estate map of only seven years earlier: south of the walled garden, the South Bower is shown for the first time, while the area to the east is described as the American Garden, also with its own bower. American gardens became a popular feature in the early nineteenth century, but paradoxically contained a wide variety of lime-hating plants from countries other than North America, particularly rhododendrons and other Ericaceae. The rows of trees shown in the earlier map have been thinned so that they appear as randomly placed specimen trees and not straight lines, making them more in keeping with the informal landscape design.

An account of the garden written in spring 1855 by Michael Saul, Head Gardener at Stourton Castle, mentions a number of exotic trees such as a large arbutus and recent introductions, for instance a Deodar (1831), Californian Redwood (*Sequoia sempervirens*, 1841), *Cryptomeria japonica* (1842) and Bhutan Cypress (*Cupressus torulosa*, 1824). In the conservatory (not the present building, although it may have been on the same site) were cinerarias, azaleas, Cape heaths, *Primula sinensis* and *Lachenalia tricolor*. A greenhouse was also stocked with flowering shrubs, perhaps to supply the conservatory, and there were also three stove houses of tropical plants, a peach house and a pine house, in which some orchids were grown alongside the pineapples. The wide range of plants grown would have been available from James Backhouse's nursery in York.

The Kitchen Garden was stocked with the choicest fruit, including a particularly good range of pear varieties such as 'Marie Louise', 'Winter Nelis', 'Easter Beurré' and 'Beurré Rance'. This was clearly a garden in which botanical diversity and the highest horticultural standards were encouraged by interested owners and made possible by highly skilled staff.

Lewis Payn Dawnay inherited the estate from his uncle in 1891; the following years saw substantial changes. In 1894 alone 11,000 trees were planted and various alterations were made to the garden and grounds. The ha-ha south of the house was curved outwards to extend the lawn; two skating ponds were made; the low wall of the North Forecourt was built and the drives realigned to allow the replanting of the North Avenue, regrettably with Broadleaved Lime, a species less tolerant of the high watertable here than the original Common Lime. The failure of many limes in the avenue has necessitated the replacement of the outer row of trees with Common Lime, the inner row being left for the time being until new trees are established.

Major-General Guy Payan Dawnay inherited Beningbrough from his father in 1910, but crippling death duties and other reasons led him to auction the property in 1916. In the absence of many family papers, the 1916 sale catalogue provides the most comprehensive insight into the estate at that time. It encompassed 33 farms, over 6,000 acres and most of the villages of Newton and Shipton. The Home Farm included a large complex of mainly nineteenth-century buildings including cowsheds, a dairy, two covered fold yards, loose boxes, stabling, pigsties, a corn house, two granaries, chicken houses, cart sheds and cottages. Other buildings within the park included the racket court built in 1901 and a castellated water tower situated on top of an artesian well on the banks of the River Ouse. It was probably built in two phases in the nineteenth century, and by 1916 an oil engine had been added to pump water up to the Hall. With its giant pillasters and castellated parapet, the tower was obviously designed to be enjoyed as a park building. The sale catalogue describes a splendid dahlia border in the walled garden slip, continuing the tradition established by Thomas Foster for growing them, and a rose garden in the area now called the Cherry Lawn.

The mansion, home farm and park were eventually bought by Lord and Lady Chesterfield in 1917. The Chesterfield Stud became the main enterprise of the estate, centred on the Home Farm, and the buildings near the Tench Pond were turned into a horse surgery.

Although they made few changes to the gardens, it seems that the Chesterfields were keen gardeners, as indicated by several plants named in their honour: Lady Chesterfield was commemorated by a carnation and a narcissus, and both she and the Earl had pelargoniums named after them; sadly, none of these seems to have survived. The Countess restored the two small formal gardens on either side of the south terrace and took particular pride in the border south of the walled garden, which was always at its best when visitors came to stay during the St Leger meeting each September.

For almost twenty years after the Trust accepted Beningbrough in 1958, it made few changes to the garden, although the Main Border was redesigned, using flowers and foliage of strong colours towards its east end grading to softer colours near the house.

When restoration of Beningbrough began in 1977, the garden was also taken in hand. The two small formal gardens, which flank the house and are enclosed by yew hedges, were redesigned. That on the west side is in the style of a sixteenth-century knot garden, with low-growing plants in hot colours, laid out between dwarf box hedges; that on the east is planted in cool colours, predominantly pale blues, pinks and silvers, arranged around a rectangular pool with a central fountain. Versailles tubs filled with plants stand on York stone paving, which alternates with areas of cobbles. New garden seats have also been provided to a traditional pattern. The nearby variegated oak was planted by the Duke of Cambridge in 1898; its new leaves, which appear in August–September, are a delicate shade of pink. The terrace terminates at its east end with an enormous Portugal Laurel. The plant has successfully layered itself and grown to a circumference of 258 feet. It is probably one of the largest laurels in the country.

The small pleasure ground west of the house was developed as an adventure playground, retaining its character as a wild garden with a circuit walk planted with evergreens and other ornamental plants. A planting scheme for the double border next to the Kitchen Garden was devised to provide colour throughout the year, but it is probably at its best in June and July, when roses, irises and paeonies are in flower. The spectacular flowers of the *Buddleja* 'Dartmoor' appear in September.

The Kitchen Garden, too labour intensive to be used for growing fruit and vegetables, is maintained as an open area for picnicking and events. The only remaining original feature is the alley of espalier pears down the centre, now edged with borders of aromatic herbs. Within the hollow walls a series of surviving pipes and flues, heated by seventeen fires, once gave off sufficient heat to protect peaches and nectarines from frost.

Hebes, *Choisya* and Purple Vine thrive against the warm south-facing wall of the South Border, which leads to the American Garden. Beds of acid soil have been introduced to the naturally alkaline ground of the American Garden to support the collection of magnolias, azaleas and rhododendrons, many of which were introduced to Britain in the early nineteenth century.

A survey in association with the Manpower Services Commission in 1986–7 mapped the estate and researched its history; trees were measured and dated, and surviving archives were examined. For the first time a more detailed picture of the development of the park and garden could be assembled, impossible from the limited and shadowy data that had previously been available. The survey revealed how the belt of trees which previously formed the boundary of the park has become sadly depleted and an extensive re-planting programme is now under way. Further planting will reinforce the existing largely informal character of the park created in the late eighteenth and early nineteenth centuries.

*(Opposite page)* *The west formal garden*

# BIBLIOGRAPHY

### BENINGBROUGH

Anon., 'Beningbrough Hall, Yorkshire', *Country Life*, xx, 1906, pp. 342–51

ARMSTRONG, James Leslie, *Beningbrough Hall: A Tale of the Eighteenth Century*, York, 1836

BEARD, Geoffrey, *Georgian Craftsmen and their Work*, 1966, pp. 24–5, 48–51 [on William Thornton]

BINNEY, Marcus, 'Beningbrough Hall Revisited', *Country Life*, clxx, 1981, pp. 1950–4, 2098–2101, 2170–3

BOTT, Alan, '*Gypsy loves Ollie 1942': A Beningbrough Story*, 1989

DRAKE, Francis, *Eboracum: or the History and Antiquities of the City of York*, 1736

FRIEDMAN, Terry F., 'A Temple Newsam Mystery Solved', *Leeds Arts Calendar*, No. 78, 1976, pp. 5–11

HALL, Ivan, 'William Thornton: A Yorkshire Borromini', *York Georgian Society Annual Report*, 1990

HATCHER, Jane, 'Beningbrough Hall, Preservation & Renewal', *York Georgian Society Annual Report*, 1980, pp. 12–15 [report of lecture by Martin Stancliffe]

JOURDAIN, Margaret, 'Furniture at Beningbrough Hall', *Country Life*, lxii, 1927, pp. 855–8

LEES-MILNE, James, *English Country Houses: Baroque*, 1970, pp. 243–51

LINSTRUM, Derek, *West Yorkshire Architects and Architecture*, 1978, pp. 61, 385 [on William Thornton]

MORRIS, M. C. F., *Yorkshire Reminiscences*, 1922, pp. 121–42 [for Payan Dawnay]

PAGE, William (ed.), *Victoria History of the North Riding*, 1923

PRICE, Stanley, and RUFFHEAD, George (ed.), *Three Yorkshire Villages: Historical Studies of Beningbrough,*

*Linton-on-Ouse and Newton-on-Ouse*, Newton-on-Ouse Local History Group, 1973

STANCLIFFE, Martin, 'Begin with Basic Principles', *Antique Collector*, li, 1980, pp. 40–3

TAYLOR, Pat, 'The Restoration Bourchiers of Beningbrough Grange', *Yorkshire Archaeological Journal*, lx, 1988, pp. 127–47

TIPPING, H. Avray, 'Beningbrough Hall', *Country Life*, lxii, 1927, pp. 772–80, 820–9

### GEORGIAN PORTRAITURE

KERSLAKE, John, *Early Georgian Portraits*, National Portrait Gallery, 1977

KERSLAKE, John, 'The National Portrait Gallery at Beningbrough', *National Trust Magazine*, Autumn 1979, pp. 8–9

KERSLAKE, John, 'The Duke of Chandos' Missing Duchess: A Portrait by Van der Mijn at Beningbrough', *National Trust Studies 1981*, 1980, pp. 139–49

PIPER, David, *Catalogue of the Seventeenth Century Portraits in the National Portrait Gallery*, Cambridge, 1963

### CHINA CLOSETS

AYERS, John, IMPEY, Oliver, *et al.*, *Porcelain for Palaces: the Fashion for Japan in Europe 1650–1750*, Oriental Ceramic Society, London, 1990

*Eastern Ceramics and Other Works of Art from the Collection of Gerald Reitlinger*, Ashmolean Museum, Oxford, 1981

HINTON, Mark, and IMPEY, Oliver, *Kakiemon: Porcelain from the English Country House*, Ashmolean Museum, Oxford, and Christie's, 1990

LANE, Arthur, 'Queen Mary's Porcelain Collection at Hampton Court Palace', *Transactions of the Oriental Ceramic Society*, xxv, 1949–50

# INDEX